DAUGHTERS OF ISRAEL
AND THEIR IMPACT IN
GOD'S KINGDOM PAST,
PRESENT AND FUTURE

RABBIN DEBORAH BRANDT

DAUGHTERS OF ISRAEL AND THEIR IMPACT IN GODS
KINGDOM PAST, PRESENT AND FUTURE

Dr. Deborah Brandt is an Ordained Rabbi with a M.Div.
Degree in Rabbinic Studies and a Ph.D. in Judaic Studies
in the Tenach and Apostolic Scriptures.
- President of Deborah's Messianic Ministries
- Rabbi/Co-Leader and Founder of The Way of
  Messiah Messianic Congregation in the Chicago
  area in Illinois, with her husband Scott Brandt
- Director and Professor with the Judaic Studies
  Institute
- Author, Teacher, Speaker
  Visit website at http://www.dmmin.org

CORRECTED TABLE OF CONTENTS

Introduction

This teaching is dedicated to all of those Women of
Valor/Eishet Chayel who are answering Gods call like
the women of old who proceeded them. God has
anointed us and called us to be wives, mothers,
intercessors and ministers, yes and even Rabbis in the
Body of Messiah, I hope this teaching blesses you as it
has blessed me.

There is a great misunderstanding on the position of
women within the Jewish Community from those
outsides of the community. It is often taught from
Christianity that Jewish woman were oppressed and not
treated with respect. However in my research I have
found that this is far from the truth. Yes, there might be
opinions of some within Judaism that would support this,
but as we will see that is not the norm.

For example, here is a quote from Everyman's Talmud
"The basis of Jewish social life is the family, and many
sections of the Talmud is ever watchful to conserve its
purity and stability. Recognizing the all-important place
which a woman occupies in the life of the family, it
accords to her a most dignified position. Especially when
her lot among the other contemporary people is taken
into account. The honor which is paid to women by the
Talmud offers a striking contrast. In no way is she
looked upon as being inferior to man, her sphere of
activity is different from man's, but of no less
significance to the welfare of the community[1]"

DAUGHTERS OF ISRAEL AND THEIR IMPACT IN GODS
KINGDOM PAST, PRESENT AND FUTURE

Rev. Martha Looper says the following in her article
"What Women Can Be and Do is Revealed by God's
Call on the life of Biblical Women". "In the Hebrew
Scriptures, there is not the slightest bent that God ever
discriminated against women. Indeed, the Holy
Scriptures themselves are the most powerful witness to
God's opportunities and giving nature and supernatural
empowerment to women for a virtual unending and
limitless range of ministries and works of service to God
and man." She goes on to say "The truth is that gender
bias in the Church has always been rooted in the
Philosophy of the Greco- Roman World, not in Holy
Scripture or in the Jewish tradition. God is consistent
throughout the Tenach and Brit HaDasha in His dealing
with women. Far from being less than men, they are
equal with men.

- In creation, they are equal.
- In Salvation, they are equal.
- In Gods gifts and graces, they are equal.

There is also an equality in proclamation so that all
women dedicated to God and his service can be used
where needed in ministry, administration, or leadership.[2]

However, women's greatest arena of ministry can and
should be their own home and children."

It is in the homes of these "Eishet Chayel"/ Women of Valor that future Apostles, Prophets, Evangelists, Rabbis and Teachers and workers of the ministry of Yeshua Ha Mashiach/Jesus the Messiah are being raised to reach the lost for the Kingdom of God.

Dr. Howard Morgan in his article "Women in Ministry, anointed for Service, Robbed of Opportunity" says the following. "The position of women in ministry has for many centuries been troubling to much of the Church. However, as we go back to our Jewish Roots, we discover that the true faith of Abraham provides both anointing and opportunity for women to fulfill their callings in the Kingdom of God. As the church departed from her Jewish Roots, she lost her understanding of the Kingdom of God and adopted the pagan understanding of "gentile authority" which Yeshua/Jesus warned us against and prohibited His disciples from emulating. This kind of authority by its nature is oppressive and repressive. It seeks to keep in power and authority those who by their military strength, political standing, or financial resources have acquired a dominant position in society. The Kingdom of God, as it is revealed in the Jewish Scriptures, is built, upon an entirely different structure. The greatest in the Kingdom of God are those who serve Matthew 23:11.[3]

Dr. John Garr of Restore Ministries says this in his article "The Biblical Women, Lessons for Today's Church from its Hebraic Heritage" "After two millennia as a new era dawned, much of Israel had been influenced by Hellenisms misogyny so that women were often

denied equal opportunity before God. Women's freedom
to minister before God was gradually withdrawn in
Second Temple Judaism. Though their material rights
were protected by the edicts of Halahcha rendered by the
sages, women found themselves more and more
restricted to home and in increasingly subservient
relationships to father and husband. The coming of
Yeshua brought a reformation of restoration to the
original intents of the Torah. Yeshua elevated women to
equality with men, so that they could sit among the
Talmudism (disciples) "at his feet" and be covered with
the dust of their Rabbi and Lord."

He goes on to say, "Though some Christian Theologians
of subsequent centuries have suggested that it is not
fitting and proper that a woman should "carry the Word
of God" He (God) arranged it so that one women carried
The Word for nine months before anyone else saw Him!
Then in another twist of irony, he also provided that the
first evangelist to proclaim the good news of the
resurrection was a woman, and a redeemed prostitute at
that!

Paul encapsulated the Messiahs position regarding
women in Christian/Messianic service. "There is….
neither male nor female, for ye are all on in Messiah
Yeshua/Christ Jesus.
And if ye be Messiahs/Christ then are ye…. heirs
according to the promise." Galatians 3:28. Men and
Women share equal rights to inherit the promises,
blessings, anointing's and appointments of Gods
Kingdom. "lech l'cha" "Get up and go" and purpose in

our hearts to leave Babylon's Gentile Traditions and go to Yerushalyim (Jerusalem) where there is freedom and equality for men and women in the biblical Hebraic Heritage of our faith"[4]

---

[1] Everyman's Talmud, p.123 Shochen publishers Abraham Cohen

[2] Rev. Martha Looper article "What Women Can Be and Do is Revealed by Gods Call on the life of Biblical Women."

[3] Dr. Howard Morgan

[4] Dr. John Garr Restore Ministry

The Uniqueness of a Woman's Soul

Why is a child considered Jewish if the mother is Jewish
and the father is not, but not considered Jewish if the
mother is Gentile and the father is Jewish? There is a
unique connection between a baby and his/her mother
due to the fact that they are connected within us for 9
months and partake of the nourishment that we have
within us and life itself.

Being Jewish, I always wondered why a child was
considered Jewish if the mother was Jewish, but not
Jewish if the woman was not Jewish? Per the scriptures,
the tribal identification was always passed down through
the fathers. However, according to some rabbinical
sources, the Rabbis decided that if a child was born of a
Jewish mother and a Gentile father that the child would
be considered Jewish. This was due to the fact that
during times of war or captivity a Jewish woman might
have been raped by a Gentile and produce a child. In
order to preserve the dignity and Jewish Heritage of the
Jewish woman and the child, they ruled that a child born
of a Jewish mother is always Jewish. [i]

According to Jewish tradition – "The essence of who
you are is from the mother".

Jewishness is not in our DNA. It is in our soul. The
reason it is passed down through the maternal line is not
just because it is easier to identify who your mother is. It
is because the soul identity is more directly shaped by
the mother than the father.

Jewishness is not in our DNA. From a purely physical
perspective, a child is more directly connected to their
mother. The father's contribution to the production of a
child is instantaneous and remote. The mother, on the
other hand, gives her very self to the child. The child is
conceived inside the mother, develops inside the mother,
is sustained and nourished by the mother, and is born
from the mother.

This is not to say that a father and child are not
intimately attached. Of course they are. But as deep and
essential as the bond between father and child may be,
the child's actual body was never a part of her father's
body. But she/he was a part of the mother. Every child
begins as an extension of their mother's body.

This is a simple fact. It doesn't mean she will be closer to
her mother, or more similar to her mother, or follow her
mother's ways. We are not discussing the emotional
bond between parent and child, but rather the natural
physical bond. There is a more direct physical link
between mother and child, because a child starts off as a
part of her mother.

The body and its workings are a mirror image of the
workings of the soul. The physical world is a parallel of
the spiritual world. And so, the direct physical link
between mother and child is a reflection of a soul link
between them. While the father's soul *contributes* to the
identity of the child's soul, it is the mother's soul that

actually *defines* it. If the mother has a Jewish soul, the
child does too.

If the mother is not Jewish but the father is, his Jewish
soul will not be extended to the child. There may be a
spark of Jewishness there, but if it was not gestated in a
Jewish mother, the child will have to go through
conversion for their Jewishness to be activated.

Jewishness is passed down by the mother because being
Jewish is a spiritual identity, it defines our very being.
And our very being we get from our mother, both in
body and in soul. Rabbi Aron Moss[1]

Brainy Sons owe Intelligence to their Mothers.

Intelligent men owe their brains to their mothers, per
research published today in The Lancet.[2]

Growing evidence shows that several genes which
determine intelligence appear to be located on the X
chromosome, the one men inherit from their mothers.
Any mutation on the X chromosome has more effect on
a man than a woman because a woman inherits X
chromosomes from both her parents, which tends to
dilute the gene's impact.

---

[1] Aron Moss is rabbi of the Nefesh Community in Sydney,
Australia, and is a frequent contributor to Chabad.org.
   [2] "Torah 101" is © 1998, 1999, 2000, 2001, 2002,
2003, 2004, 2005, 2006, 2007, 2008, 2009, 2010, 2011, 2012
by Mechon Mamre, 12 Hayyim Vital St., Jerusalem,
Israel. 972-2-652-1906 last updated: 24 January 2012

But a man only has one X chromosome inherited from his mother, which is paired with the much smaller Y chromosomes from his father. Therefore, an intelligence-enhancing X gene has more of a chance of becoming the predominate gene, determining the man's basic intelligence, looks and character. It also works the other way; if the predominate gene is not as strong as it should be Developmentally delayed.

Professor Gillian Turner, the author of the study, said: "If the gene is the one that increases intelligence, then its full effect will be seen in men, while in women the benefit is less pronounced. This explains why some men are extraordinarily intelligent." She concludes that if a man wants smart sons his best bet is to marry a smart woman. LENDA COOPER

Women's Spirituality.

Women in many ways are more naturally spiritually in tune to God then men. This is why men and women need each other, what one lacks the other makes up for. Women in general see things that men do not see. Women are naturally at a higher spiritual level then men (Rabbi Ken Spiro)

Daughters of Israel – Women's Impact in Biblical History

It is impossible to write about every woman in the Bible in this short chapter on Women's Impact in Biblical History, however I am going to pick out the ones who have inspired me in my walk and call as a woman and Rabbi. I hope that they will inspire you as well. The ones I have chosen, who I felt made a major impact as daughters of Israel in God's plans and purpose in Biblical History, are Eve, Sarah, Rebecca, Rachel & Leah, Jael and Deborah.

Macon Mamre -According to traditional Judaism, women are endowed with a greater degree of "binah" (intuition, understanding, intelligence) than men. The rabbis inferred this from the idea that women was "built" (Genesis 2,22) rather than "formed" (Genesis 2,7), and the Hebrew root of "build" has the same consonants as the word "binah". It has been said that the matriarchs (Sarah, Rebecca, Rachel, and Leah) were superior to the patriarchs (Abraham, Isaac, and Jacob) in prophecy. It has also been said that women did not participate in the idolatry regarding the golden calf. Some traditional sources suggest that women are closer to God's ideal than men.[3]

---

[3] "Torah 101" is © 1998, 1999, 2000, 2001, 2002, 2003, 2004, 2005, 2006, 2007, 2008, 2009, 2010, 2011, 2012 by Mechon Mamre, 12 Hayyim Vital St., Jerusalem, Israel. 972-2-652-1906 last updated: 24 January 2012

Women have held positions of respect in Judaism since biblical times. Miriam is considered one of the liberators of the people of Israel, along with her brothers Moses and Aaron. One of the Judges (Deborah) was a woman. Seven of the 55 prophets of the Bible were women.

The Rabbis taught in *Megillah* (14a), one of the tractates of the Talmud, that there were seven prophetesses in Israel: "Our Rabbis taught: Forty-eight prophets and seven prophetesses prophesied to Israel . . .. 'Seven prophetesses. Who were these? – Sarah, Miriam, Deborah, Hannah, Abigail, Huldah and Esther."[ii] (See end note)

The Impact of Eve/Chavah – The Mother of all Mankind

Of course, we need to start with Eve/Chavah, the mother of us all. The impact of her disobeying YHWH has truly affected and has had impact on every human being born on the face of the earth.

She is also the "model" that is used to continue the lie, "you can't trust a woman, remember what Eve/Chavah did" or "It's the women's fault we are in this mess". Well, you are 50% correct blaming the disobedience to YHVH's word on her, but remember Adam was right there and did not do what he was supposed to do, protect his wife from the enemy and be the spiritual leader. The instruction was given directly to Adam, then Adam passed it onto his wife Chavah.

Yes, as women we have inherited the curses as stated in Genesis 3 due to her rebellion. However, in Messiah Yeshua, He has reversed the curse as He restored women to a place of dignity and leadership that was lost back in the Garden. This is not to say that we no longer have an easy road, but we can do all things through Messiah Yeshua who gives us strength. Phil 4:13

There is no doubt we are the weaker vessel physically but not spiritually. 11 Cor. 12:9.

Eve/Chavah paid dearly in her life along with Adam due to this disobedience, they felt, experienced and witnessed the results of disobeying God till the day they

died. But they also experienced the love, grace, mercy
and forgiveness of God as well and past that on to their
offspring.

Here is a quote from the Women of Destiny Bible[4]

Eve (or her Hebrew name Chavah) was the original first
lady. She was not only a woman's first experience with
God, but God's first experience with a woman. She was
the first to delight the Father's heart as only a daughter
can. She was the first to grace this Earth with the ways
of a woman and the first to encounter the wiles of the
devil/hasatan. She was the first to love a man and the
first to mislead one. She was the first to try to hide from
God and the first to break His heart with her sin. She
was the first to bear-and the first to bury-a child. She was
the first to know the love of God and the first to suffer
the curse of fallen humanity. She was the one after whom
every woman who has ever lived has follow.

You too are a daughter of God. You were created and
called according to His purpose. He may be calling you,
live Eve/Chavah to pioneer. His destiny for your life
may include some unexplored or unexpected territory. So
go boldly after Him. Follow Him with all your heart.
And if He asks you to do for Him what has not been
done before, remember Eve/Chavah. She had no mentor,
no mother, no older female friend to help her on her way.
She had only God; and if you ever find yourself as a first

---

[4] Women of Destiny Bible Thomas Nelson Publishers copyright
2000

lady, He will be there to help you blaze every trail and break open each new day.

As I read the above quote, I thought of all the women of the "Messianic Movement", like myself who are trying to find their place as His Torah obedient daughters in the Body of Messiah. Many of us had many friends in the Church, then we rediscovered our Hebrew Roots and made a choice to follow the Torah and not the traditions of men and soon found ourselves alone in the wilderness, learning to trust His guidance and provision for our lives, even if it meant walking alone for a season. But YHWH if faithful and He will use us if we are willing to be all He has called us to be in these last days.

As we study about these Virtuous Women who have gone before us, I pray that we will be strengthened and encouraged to know that we can do all things through Messiah who strengthens us. Philippians 4:13

A Suitable Helpmeet named Woman.

Gen 2:20 The man gave names to all livestock, and to the birds of the sky, and to every animal of the field; but for man there was not found a helper suitable for him.

The Hebrew word for "Help" is "Ezer"

Strong's #H5828
עֵזֶר
ʽêzer
ayʹ-zer

From H5826; *aid:* - help.
1) help, succor
1a) help, succor
1b) one who helps

Gen 2:21 And the LORD God caused a deep sleep to fall
upon Adam, and he slept: and he took one of his ribs,
and closed up the flesh instead thereof;
Gen 2:22 And the rib, which the LORD God had taken
from man, made he a woman, and brought her unto the
man.
Gen 2:23 And Adam said, This *is* now bone of my bones,
and flesh of my flesh: she shall be called Women,
because she was taken out of Man.

Only a woman is a suitable helper "Ezer" for the
Man. As the saying goes, God made Adam for Eve, not
Adam for Steve. Our husbands need us, just like we
need them. We have what they are missing, and they
have what we are missing, but together we are
complete. Adam was complete, out of Adam came the
Women. When a man and women marry, they become
"One Flesh" just as Adam was one flesh with Chavah.

Here is what the Chumash Torah Commentary says
regarding vs. 18[5]

---

[5] The Chumash, The Stone Edition, Art Scroll Series Published by
Mesorah Publications ltd copyright 1998, 2000

"A helper corresponding to him" (lit a helper against him). If the man is worthy, the women will be a helper, if he is unworthy she will be against him (Yavamos 63a, Rashi). Many have noted that the ideal marriage is not necessarily one of total agreement in all matters. Often it is the wife's responsibility to oppose her husband and prevent him from acting rashly, or to help him achieve a common course by questioning, criticizing and discussing. Thus, the verse means literally that there are times when a wife can best be a helper by being against him"

When would it be an appropriate time to "go or be against him" the husband and be a helper that God called you to be? When he is or is going to do something that will harm His relationship with God and His Torah, himself and/or his family. There are times when we as women, wives and mothers must take a stand for His Torah to be upheld in our homes. We do this by prayer and studying his Torah[3], by being a submissive wife and by helping our husband become all God has created him to be and to oppose anything that would destroy the Shalom of our home or come between us and our relationship with God and Our Messiah Yeshua. – Psalm 1

H802 – Women
נשׁים אשּׁה
'ishshâh nâshîym
ish-shaw', naw-sheem'
The first form is the feminine of H376 or H582; the second form is an irregular plural; a woman (used in the

same wide sense as H582).: - [adulter]ess, each, every, female, X many, + none, one, + together, wife, women. Often unexpressed in English.

Gen 2:24 Therefore shall a man leave his father and his mother, and shall cleave unto his wife: and they shall be one flesh.

Chumash – "One Flesh" Let him cling to his wife and to none other, because man and wife are in reality one flesh, as they were at the beginning of Creation. But that can happen only if they also become one mind, one heart, one soul…and if they subordinate all their strength and effort to the service of God.

Gen 2:25 And they were both naked, the man and his wife, and were not ashamed.

Chumash[6]

'The Torah mentions this as an indication of the purity of Adam and Eve. People are ashamed of their nakedness because they associate vileness and lust with their private parts. But not Adam and Eve. As Stomo explains, they used all their organs exclusively to do God's will, not to satisfy their personal desires. To them, even cohabitation was as innocent as eating and drinking, so they had no reason to cover their bodies".

---

[6] The Chumash, The Stone Edition, Art Scroll Series Published by Mesorah Publications ltd copyright 1998, 2000

YHWH's glory was their covering and there was no
shame. Sin brings shame. Before Man/Adam fell they
were not ashamed.

Chavah meets the "Deceiver"

Deceive
DECE'IVE, v.t. [L to take asid, to ensnare.]

1. To mislead the mind; to cause to err; to cause to
believe what is false, or disbelieve what is true; to
impose on; to delude.

Take heed that no man deceives you. Mat 24.

If we say we have no sin, we deceive ourselves. 1 John
1.

2. To beguile; to cheat.

Your father hath deceived me, and changed my wages
ten times.

3. To cut off from expectation; to frustrate or disappoint;
as, his hopes were deceived.

4. To take from; to rob.

Gen 3:1 Now the serpent was more subtle than any
beast of the field which the LORD God had made. And

he said unto the women, Yea, hath God said, Ye shall not
eat of every tree of the garden?

What is the first thing that is planted into Chavah's
ear? Doubt! Doubt that YHWH's Torah, His Word can
be trusted. The enemy's tactic is the same today, he
wants us to question God's faithfulness and His promises
for our life and family. He wants us to question our
mate's ability to take care of us, he wants us to doubt our
ability to be a good wife and mother, he wants us to
question the gifts and callings YHWH has put upon our
lives as well. HE IS A LIER AND THE FATHER OF
LIES!!

 2Co 11:3 But I am afraid that somehow, as the
serpent deceived Chavah in his craftiness, your minds
might be corrupted from the simplicity that is in
Messiah.

The enemy wants to deceive us in order to corrupt our
minds into thinking that YHWH made a mistake when
He made us. Those who fall for the lies that "Women's
Lib" have fed the world have had their minds
corrupted. We have true liberation in Messiah as His
daughters. Ha Satan wants us to be deceived in thinking
that YHWH can't use us, or to listen to the lie that
because of what Chavah did we, as women are doomed
to be second class citizens.

2Co 11:14 And no wonder, for even ha Satan
masquerades as an angel of light.

In what ways could he deceive the Bride of Messiah and
The Church? Here are some of the lies that he has
planted, and Christians have taken as the truth when it
was a lie and deception and my response to his lies

1.   The Church has replaced Israel

2.   We do not have to keep the Torah, it is bondage

3.   We do not have to keep the Biblical feasts, they are
only for the Jewish people

4.   The Sabbath was changed to Sunday; we are not to
keep the 7th day Sabbath

5.   The new holidays that replaced YHWH'S feasts
are, Christmas, Easter and Halloween

6.   The Old Testament has been done away with, we
only need to read the Epistles of Paul everything
else does not apply.

The list can go on and on. None of the above have any
scriptural basis, yet Christians have accepted them as
'Gospel Truth". And because they have no foundation
in the Torah they are easily deceived and are thrown
about by every wind of doctrine.

Rev 12:9 The great dragon was thrown down, the old
serpent, he who is called the devil and Hasatan, the
deceiver of the whole world. He was thrown down to the
earth, and his angels were thrown down with him.(TLV)

Ha Satan is the TEMPTOR, not YHWH

Jam 1:12 Blessed *is* the man that endureth temptation:
for when he is tried, he shall receive the crown of life,
which the Lord hath promised to them that love him.
Jam 1:13 Let no man say when he is tempted, I am
tempted of God: for God cannot be tempted with evil,
neither tempteth he any man:
Jam 1:14 But every man is tempted, when he is drawn
away of his own lust, and enticed.
Jam 1:15 Then when lust hath conceived, it bringeth
forth sin: and sin, when it is finished, bringeth forth
death. (KJV)

Isn't this a picture of what happened to Chavah. The
tempter came, instead of fleeing or standing against the
temptation; she was drawn away by her own lust and
enticed.   Once that lust was conceived (or given life by
action) it brought forth sin into the world, which brought
forth death.

Jam 1:16 Do not err, my beloved brethren.
Jam 1:17 Every good gift and every perfect gift is from
above, and cometh down from the Father of lights, with
whom is no variableness, neither shadow of turning.
Jam 1:18 Of his own will begat he us with the word of
truth, that we should be a kind of first fruits of his
creatures.
Jam 1:19 Wherefore, my beloved brethren, let every
man be swift to hear, slow to speak, slow to wrath

Jam 1:20 For the wrath of man worketh not the
righteousness of God.
Jam 1:21 Wherefore lay apart all filthiness and
superfluity of naughtiness, and receive with meekness
the engrafted word, which is able to save your souls.
Jam 1:22 But be ye doers of the word, and not hearers
only, deceiving your own selves. (KJV)

If we are not being a doer of His Torah then we are
deceiving ourselves just like Chavah was deceived.

Jam 1:23 For if any be a hearer of the word, and not a
doer, he is like unto a man beholding his natural face in a
glass:
Jam 1:24 For he beholdeth himself, and goeth his way,
and straightway forgetteth what manner of man he was.
Jam 1:25 But whoso looketh into the perfect law of
liberty, and continueth *therein*, he being not a forgetful
hearer, but a doer of the work, this man shall be blessed
in his deed.
Jam 1:26 If any man among you seem to be religious,
and bridleth not his tongue, but deceiveth his own heart,
this man's religion *is* vain.
Jam 1:27 Pure religion and undefiled before God and
the Father is this, To visit the fatherless and widows in
their affliction, *and* to keep himself unspotted from the
world. (KJV)

What did Yeshua do when he was tempted by Ha Satan,
He spoke forth the Torah, YHWH's teaching and
instructions. He did not listen to the enemies twisting of
the truth (the same way he twisted the truth to Chavah),

or allow him to plant any doubts into His mind he simply spoke what YHWH truly had said and did not add or take away from the Torah.

Mat 4:1 Then Yeshua was led up by the Spirit into the wilderness to be tempted by the devil.

Mat 4:2 When he had fasted forty days and forty nights, he was hungry afterward.

Mat 4:3 The tempter came and said to him, "If you are the Son of God, command that these stones become bread."

Mat 4:4 But he answered, "It is written, 'Man shall not live by bread alone, but by every word that proceeds out of the mouth of God.'"

Mat 4:5 Then the devil took him into the holy city. He set him on the pinnacle of the temple,

Mat 4:6 and said to him, "If you are the Son of God, throw yourself down, for it is written, 'He will give his angels charge concerning you.' and, 'On their hands they will bear you up, so that you don't dash your foot against a stone.'"

Mat 4:7 Yeshua said to him, "Again, it is written, 'You shall not test the Lord, your God.'"

Mat 4:8 Again, the devil took him to an exceedingly high mountain, and showed him all the kingdoms of the world, and their glory.

Mat 4:9 He said to him, "I will give you all of these things, if you will fall down and worship me."

Mat 4:10 Then Yeshua said to him, "Get behind me, Hasatan! For it is written, 'You shall worship the Lord your God, and him only shall you serve.'"

DAUGHTERS OF ISRAEL AND THEIR IMPACT IN GODS
KINGDOM PAST, PRESENT AND FUTURE

Mat 4:11 Then the devil left him, and behold, angels
came and served him. (TLV)

We stand against the enemies lies and deceit by studying
and speaking forth His Torah as Yeshua did.

1Ti 2:13 For Adam was first formed, then Chavah.
1Ti 2:14 Adam wasn't deceived, but the women, being
deceived, has fallen into disobedience;(CJB)

Note what it says here, Adam was <u>not deceived</u>, he knew
the enemy was lying to Chavah, He knew what YHWH
had told him regarding the tree and the garden because
the instructions were given directly to him.   He failed to
be Chavah's protector and followed her lead instead of
rebuking the deceiver. Chavah failed to look to Adam to
ask if what the deceiver was saying was true. Adam
followed his wife's lead, instead of Chavah looking to
him. Here we see the first marriage getting out of divine
order with dire results.

1Ti 2:15 but she will be saved through her childbearing,
if they continue in faith, love, and sanctification with
sobriety. (TLV)

The enemy wants us to fall into disobedience to His
Torah, so that we will miss out on what YHWH has
called us to do. He wants us to become rebellious
against our husbands and His perfect plan for marriage
and make us think that the grass is greener on the other
side, when it is really all burnt up! YHWH is calling us
In Yeshua to walk continuously in faith, love,

sanctification and sobriety as His virtuous women in these last days.

Gen 3:2 And the women said unto the serpent, We may eat of the fruit of the trees of the garden:
Gen 3:3 But of the fruit of the tree which *is* in the midst of the garden, God hath said, Ye shall not eat of it, neither shall ye touch it, lest ye die. (KJV)

Chavah misquotes what YHWH has said. Are we being good students of His Torah so that when the enemy tries to deceive us we know, that we know that we know what YHWH has said and not add or take away from His Torah?

Gen 3:4 And the serpent said unto the women, Ye shall not surely die:
Gen 3:5 For God doth know that in the day ye eat thereof, then your eyes shall be opened, and ye shall be as gods, knowing good and evil. (KJV)

Again, the deceiver makes Chavah doubt YHWH's Torah, His Word and His Character.

Gen 3:6 And when the women saw that the tree *was* good for food, and that it *was* pleasant to the eyes, and a tree to be desired to make *one* wise, she took of the fruit thereof, and did eat, and gave also unto her husband with her; and he did eat. (KJV)

The Women "Saw", Pleasant to the eyes" "A Tree to be Desired" – beware what you allow your eyes to look at so that it doesn't turn into the lust of the flesh. Are you meditating on the latest "Romance Novel" or on His Torah? What kind of fruit are you growing in your life? Galatians 5

Chumash[7]

"For God knows" The serpent used another ploy familiar to those who try to rationalize the Torah away. They contend that those who convey and interpret the Law of God are motivated by a selfish desire to consolidate power in themselves. "God did not prohibit this tree out of any concern for your lives, but because He is aware that by eating from it you will attain extra wisdom and become omniscient like Him. Then you will be independent of Him" (R. Hirsh). The tempter did not explicitly tell the women to eat the fruit, but he had enveloped her in his spell. She looked on the tree with a new longing.... Its' fruit was good to eat, a delight to the eyes, and it would give her wisdom. Then she brought it to Adam and repeated everything the serpent had told her. He was "At one with her" and not blameless (i.e. he was not hopelessly tempted or unreasonably deceived) and therefore liable to punishment) (Radak; ibn Ezra)

Gen 3:7 And the eyes of them both were opened, and they knew that they *were* naked; and they sewed fig leaves together, and made themselves aprons.
Gen 3:8 And they heard the voice of the LORD God walking in the garden in the cool of the day: and Adam

---

[7] The Chumash, The Stone Edition, Art Scroll Series Published by Mesorah Publications ltd copyright 1998, 2000

and his wife hid themselves from the presence of the
LORD God amongst the trees of the garden.

Gen 3:9 And the LORD God called unto Adam, and said
unto him, Where *art* thou?

Gen 3:10 And he said, I heard thy voice in the garden,
and I was afraid, because I *was* naked; and I hid myself.

Gen 3:11 And he said, Who told thee that
thou *wast* naked? Hast thou eaten of the tree, whereof I
commanded thee that thou shouldest not eat?

Gen 3:12 And the man said, The women whom thou
gavest *to be* with me, she gave me of the tree, and I did
eat.

Gen 3:13 And the LORD God said unto the women,
What *is* this *that* thou hast done? And the women said,
The serpent beguiled me, and I did eat.

Gen 3:14 And the LORD God said unto the serpent,
Because thou hast done this, thou *art* cursed above all
cattle, and above every beast of the field; upon thy belly
shalt thou go, and dust shalt thou eat all the days of thy
life:

Gen 3:15 And I will put enmity between thee and the
women, and between thy seed and her seed; it shall
bruise thy head, and thou shalt bruise his heel.

Gen 3:16 Unto the women he said, I will greatly
multiply thy sorrow and thy conception; in sorrow thou
shalt bring forth children; and thy desire *shall be* to thy
husband, and he shall rule over thee. (KJV)

Chumash [8]

*"Before the sin, Adam and Eve lived together and she
conceived and gave birth immediately and painlessly.
Now that would change. Conception would not be
automatic, and there would be an extended period of
pregnancy and labor pains. (Sforno)*

*" And he shall rule over you" Her punishment was
measure for measure. She influenced her husband to eat
at her command: now she would become subservient to
him (Ramban). The new conditions of life that made
sustenance the product of hard labor would naturally
make women dependent on the physically stronger men.
Obedience to Torah; however; restores her to her former
and proper status as the crown of her husband and pearl
of his life (Proverbs 12:4. 31:10) R. Hirsh*

*The Sages ordained that a man should honor his wife
more than himself, and love her as himself. If he has
money, he should increase his generosity to her
according to his means. He should not cast fear upon her
unduly and his conversation with her should be gentle,
he should be prone neither to melancholy nor anger.
They have similarly ordained that a wife should honor
her husband exceedingly and revere him… and refrain
from anything that is repugnant to him. This is the way of
the daughter of Israel who are holy and pure in their*

---

[8] The Chumash, The Stone Edition, Art Scroll
Series Published by Mesorah Publications ltd copyright
1998, 2000

*union, and in these ways will their life together be
seemly and praiseworthy (Rambam Hil. Ishus 15:19-20)*

Eph 5:22 Wives, be subject to your own husbands, as to
the Lord.

Eph 5:23 For the husband is the head of the wife, and
Messiah also is the head of the assembly, being himself
the savior of the body.

Eph 5:24 But as the assembly is subject to Messiah, so
let the wives also be to their own husbands in
everything.

Eph 5:25 Husbands, love your wives, even as Messiah
also loved the assembly, and gave himself up for it;

Eph 5:26 that he might sanctify it, having cleansed it by
the washing of water with the word,

Eph 5:27 that he might present the assembly to himself
gloriously, not having spot or wrinkle or any such thing;
but that it should be holy and without blemish.

Eph 5:28 Even so husbands also ought to love their own
wives as their own bodies. He who loves his own wife
loves himself.

Eph 5:29 For no man ever hated his own flesh; but
nourishes and cherishes it, even as the Lord also does the
assembly;

Eph 5:30 because we are members of his body, of his
flesh and bones.

Eph 5:31 "For this cause a man will leave his father and
mother, and will be joined to his wife. The two will
become one flesh."

Eph 5:32 This mystery is great, but I speak concerning
Messiah and of the assembly.

Eph 5:33 Nevertheless each of you must also love his own wife even as himself; and let the wife see that she respects her husband. (CJB)

Gen 3:17 And unto Adam he said, Because thou hast hearkened unto the voice of thy wife, and hast eaten of the tree, of which I commanded thee, saying, Thou shalt not eat of it: cursed *is* the ground for thy sake; in sorrow shalt thou eat *of* it all the days of thy life; (KJV)

Chumash [9]
"People always make choices in life and they are responsible for them. Adam failed to exercise his responsibility to investigate what he was being offered and to realize that when he had to choose between pleasing God and pleasing the one who was offering a momentarily enticing choice, his first allegiance had to be to God. As or HaCahaim put it, he succumbed to her voice without examining the content of her words."

Gen 3:18 Thorns also and thistles shall it bring forth to thee; and thou shalt eat the herb of the field;
Gen 3:19 In the sweat of thy face shalt thou eat bread, till thou return unto the ground; for out of it wast thou taken: for dust thou *art*, and unto dust shalt thou return.
Gen 3:20 And Adam called his wife's name Eve; because she was the mother of all living. (KJV)

---

[9] The Chumash, The Stone Edition, Art Scroll Series
Published by Mesorah Publications ltd copyright 1998, 2000

H2332 - Eve

חוּה

Chavah

khav-vaw'

Causative from H2331; *lifegiver*; *Chavvah* (or Eve), the
first women: - Eve.

Chumash – Her name indicates she is the mother of all the living.

Gen 3:21 Unto Adam also and to his wife did the LORD
God make coats of skins, and clothed them.
Gen 3:22 And the LORD God said, Behold, the man is
become as one of us, to know good and evil: and now,
lest he put forth his hand, and take also of the tree of life,
and eat, and live forever:
Gen 3:23 Therefore the LORD God sent him forth from
the garden of Eden, to till the ground from whence he
was taken.
Gen 3:24 So he drove out the man; and he placed at the
east of the garden of Eden Cherubim's, and a flaming
sword which turned every way, to keep the way of the
tree of life. (KJV)

Chumash
*"God grieved at the sin and its results for Adam had now
made it impossible for God to let him stay in the garden.
By eating from the Tree of Knowledge, Man had become
like the "Unique One among us", meaning that he had
become unique among the terrestrial ones, just as God is
unique among the celestial ones, for now Man can
discriminate between good and bad, a quality not*

possessed by cattle and beasts (Rashi, following Targum). Because Man has this unique ability to know good and evil, and his desire for sensual gratification had become enhanced, there was a new danger. If Man kept the capacity to live forever, he might well spend all his days pursuing gratification and cast away intellectual growth and good deeds. He would fail to attain the spiritual bliss that God intended for him. If so, Man had to be banished from Eden, so that he would not be able to eat from the Tree of Life and live forever."[10]

Chavah along with Adam paid dearly for that time she chooses to listen to the deceiver. However out of the fall came great mercy and grace, Messiah Yeshua.

Batya Wooten writes in her book "Mama's Torah, the Role of Women"[11]

"Eve ate of the forbidden fruit and it was thereafter decreed of all of her daughters, "Your desire shall be toward your husband, and he shall rule over you" Genesis 3:16

Like the "by the sweat of your brow" curse pronounced over her husband, so "ruling over the women" is part of the women's curse for disobedience."

---

[10] The Chumash, The Stone Edition, Art Scroll Series Published by Mesorah Publications ltd copyright 1998, 2000

[11] Mama's Torah The Role of Women by Batya Ruth Wootten, Key of David Publishers copyright 2004 Batya Wootten

This ruling could not have been part of the original plan
for our lives since it was decreed as part of our
punishment. This is instead a product of sin, and thus
should not be commended as though it were an ideal, for
those who follow the Messiah are no longer under the
curse" (Galatians 3:10)

Do not let the enemy rob you of the blessings that
YHWH has planned for you and your family by listening
to his lies. Choose this day not to be deceived as Chavah
was, learn from her and choose the path of life, the path
of the way of His Torah.

Jos 1:6 Be strong and of good courage; for you shall
cause this people to inherit the land which I swore to
their fathers to give them.
Jos 1:7 Only be strong and very courageous, to observe
to do according to all the law, which Moshe my servant
commanded you. Don't turn from it to the right hand or
to the left, that you may have good success wherever you
go.
Jos 1:8 This scroll of the Torah shall not depart out of
your mouth, but you shall meditate on it day and night,
that you may observe to do according to all that is
written therein: for then you shall make your way
prosperous, and then you shall have good success.
Jos 1:9 Haven't I commanded you? Be strong and of
good courage. Don't be afraid, neither be dismayed: for
the LORD your God is with you wherever you go. (CJB)

Jos 24:15 If it seem evil to you to serve the LORD, choose you this day whom you will serve; whether the gods which your fathers served that were beyond the River, or the gods of the Amori, in whose land you dwell: but as for me and my house, we will serve the LORD.
(KJV)

The Impact of Sarah – The Mother of Israel

Sarah's Profile in A Nutshell

Strengths and accomplishments
- Was intensely loyal to her own child.
- Became the mother of a nation and an ancestor of Yeshua.
- Was a woman of faith, the first women listed in Hebrews 11 Hall of Faith

Weakness and mistakes
- Has trouble believing God's promise to her.
- Attempted to work problems out on her own, without consulting God.
- Tried to cover her faults by blaming others.

Lessons from her life
- God responds to faith even in the midst of failure.
- God is not bound by what usually happens; he can stretch the limits and cause unheard-of events to occur.

Vital Statistics
- Married Abram in Ur of the Chaldeans, then moved with him to Canaan.
- Occupation: Wife, mother, household manager
- Relatives: Father; Terah, Husband; Abraham, Half-brothers; Nahor and Haran. Nephew: Lot son; Isaac

Key Verses
Sarah's story is told in Genesis/B'rysheet 11 to 25. She is
also mentioned in Isaiah 51:2, Romans 4:19; Romans
9:9, Hebrews 11:11; 1 Peter 3:6

Even at 90 Sarah was considered a beautiful woman and
loved and respected by her husband Abraham. The only
thing that was missing was a child that they were beyond
hope of having. However, God had other plans and Sarah
became the mother of a nation, the nation of Israel.

Sarah was a woman of Divine Inspiration, Vision and
Dominion. When God called Abram He also called
Sarah. She had a long wait for her dream of a child to
manifest from the time she was married to Abraham until
Isaac's birth, however she persevered. She made a
mistake in underestimating that God's promise would
come from her womb, not that of Hagar, but the promise
was fulfilled despite her trying to help God. Sarah is a
Eishet Chayel, an example for all women to follow. Full
of grace and beauty and submitted to God's will. She
was a woman of faith and strength. Both her and
Abraham had to believe the impossible, walk in
obedience to God's instructions, leave what was known
for what was not known. Sarah had to see with spiritual
eyes what could not be seen in the natural. Strength and
dignity were her clothing. Her physical beauty was only
surpassed by her spiritual beauty.

Genesis 11:29 And Abram and Nahor took them wives:
the name of Abram's wife *was* Sarai; and the name of

Nahor's wife, Milcah, the daughter of Haran, the father
of Milcah, and the father of Iscah.
Gen 11:30 But Sarai was barren; she *had* no child.
(KJV)

Iscah: This is Sarah [called Iscah] because she would see
(סוֹכָה) through Divine inspiration, and because all gazed
(סוֹכִין) at her beauty. Alternatively, יִסְכָּה is an expression
denoting princedom, (נְסִיכוּת), just as Sarah is an
expression of dominion (שְׂרָרָה) . - [from Meg. 14a]

Gen 12:1 Now the LORD had said unto Abram, Get
thee out of thy country, and from thy kindred, and from
thy father's house, unto a land that I will shew thee:
Gen 12:2 And I will make of thee a great nation, and I
will bless thee, and make thy name great; and thou shalt
be a blessing: (KJV)

Sarah was a teacher of Torah, just as Abram. She would
teach the women the ways of the God of Abram based
on the Torah/Teachings and Instructions that were
revealed to them at that time. [12]

Gen 12:3 And I will bless them that bless thee, and
curse him that curseth thee: and in thee shall all families
of the earth be blessed.
Gen 12:4 So Abram departed, as the LORD had spoken
unto him; and Lot went with him: and Abram *was*
seventy and five years old when he departed out of
Haran.

---

[12] http://www.mechon-mamre.org/jewfaq/women.htm The
Role of Women

Gen 12:5 And Abram took Sarai his wife, and Lot his
brother's son, and all their substance that they had
gathered, and the souls that they had gotten in Haran;
and they went forth to go into the land of Canaan; and
into the land of Canaan they came. (KJV)

According to Rabbinic Commentary "And the souls
they had acquired in Haran: whom he had brought under
the wings of the Shechinah. Abraham would convert the
men, and Sarah would convert the women, and Scripture
ascribes to them [a merit] as if they had made them
(Gen. Rabbah 39:14). (Hence, the expression אֲשֶׁר עָשׂוּ,
lit. that they made.) The simple meaning of the verse is:
the slaves and maidservants that they had acquired for
themselves, as in [the verse] (below 31:1): "He acquired
(עָשָׂה) all this wealth" [an expression of acquisition];
(Num. 24:18): "and Israel acquires," an expression of
acquiring and gathering. (Rashi Commentary Gen. 12:5)

Hagar was the daughter of Pharaoh and when he saw the
blessings that were upon Sarah, he allowed his daughter
to become Sarah's handmaiden in hopes she would be
blessed as well. (Rashi Commentary)

Gen 16:1 Now Sarai Abram's wife bare him no children:
and she had an handmaid, an Egyptian, whose name *was*
Hagar.
Gen 16:2 And Sarai said unto Abram, Behold now, the
LORD hath restrained me from bearing: I pray thee, go
in unto my maid; it may be that I may obtain children by
her. And Abram hearkened to the voice of Sarai.

Gen 16:3 And Sarai Abram's wife took Hagar her maid
the Egyptian, after Abram had dwelt ten years in the land
of Canaan, and gave her to her husband Abram to be his
wife.
Gen 16:4 And he went in unto Hagar, and she
conceived: and when she saw that she had conceived, her
mistress was despised in her eyes.
Gen 16:5 And Sarai said unto Abram, My wrong *be*
upon thee: I have given my maid into thy bosom; and
when she saw that she had conceived, I was despised in
her eyes: the LORD judge between me and thee. (KJV)

"an Egyptian handmaid: She was Pharaoh's daughter.
When he (Pharaoh) saw the miracles that were wrought
for Sarah, he said, "It is better that my daughter be a
handmaid in this household, then a mistress in another
household." - [from Gen. Rabbah 45:1]

Sarah change of status from "My Princess' to "Princess
over all". God not only exalts her status but also renews
her body to that of her youth.

Genesis 17:15-19 And God said unto Abraham, As for
Sarai thy wife, thou shalt not call her name Sarai, but
Sarah *shall* her name *be. (KJV)*

"you shall not call her name Sarai: which means "my
princess," for me, but not for others. But Sarah, in an
unqualified sense, shall be her name, that she will be a
princess over all. "— [from Ber. 13a] Rashi

And I will bless her: And what is the blessing? That she
returned to her youth, as it is said (below 18:12): "My
skin has become smooth." - [from B.M. 87a] Rashi

Even at age 90, God would bless her with the ability of a
young women in order to nurse her son.

And I will bless her, and give thee a son also of her: yea,
I will bless her, and she shall be *a mother* of nations;
kings of people shall be of her.

"and I will bless her: with breast feeding, when she
required it, on the day of Isaac's feast, for people were
murmuring against them, that they had brought a
foundling from the street and were saying, "He is our
son." So each one brought her child with her, but not her
wet nurse, and she (Sarah) nursed them all. That is what
is said (below 21:7): "Sarah has nursed children." Gen.
Rabbah (53:9) alludes slightly to this." — [from B.M.
87a] Rashi

Then Abraham fell upon his face, and laughed, and said
in his heart, Shall *a child* be born unto him that is an
hundred years old? and shall Sarah, that is ninety years
old, bear?
And Abraham said unto God, O that Ishmael might live
before thee!
And God said, Sarah thy wife shall bear thee a son
indeed; and thou shalt call his name Isaac: and I will
establish my covenant with him for an everlasting
covenant, *and* with his seed after him.

Gen 18:10 And he said, I will certainly return unto thee
according to the time of life; and, lo, Sarah thy wife shall
have a son. And Sarah heard *it* in the tent door, which
was behind him.
Gen 18:11 Now Abraham and Sarah *were* old *and* well
stricken in age; *and* it ceased to be with Sarah after the
manner of women.
Gen 18:12 Therefore Sarah laughed within herself,
saying, After I am waxed old shall I have pleasure, my
lord being old also? (KJV)

"I will surely return: The angel did not announce that he
[himself] would return to him, but he was speaking to
him as an emissary of the Omnipresent. Similarly,
(above 16:10): "And the angel said to her: I will greatly
multiply [your seed]," but he [the angel] did not have the
power to multiply [her children], but he spoke as an
emissary of the Omnipresent. Here too, it was as an
emissary of the Omnipresent that he said this to him.
(Elisha said to the Shunamite women (II Kings 4:16):
"At this season, at this time next year, you will be
embracing a son." And she said, "No my lord, O man of
God, do not fail your maidservant. Those angels who
announced to Sarah said (below verse 14): 'At the
appointed time, I will return,'" [but Elisha did not
promise to return]. Elisha replied, "Those angels, who
live and endure forever, said, 'At the appointed time, I
will return.' But I am flesh and blood, alive today and
dead tomorrow. Whether I shall be alive or dead, 'At this
time, etc. [you will embrace a son.'"] (Gen. Rabbah
53:2)"

When Ishmael became a threat to Isaac and Sarah was concerned about her son's welfare, God came to Sarah's defense and cast Hagar and Ishmael away from the son of promise in order to protect him and Sarah. Sarah was a woman of much wisdom and saw that Ishmael was abusing her son and that to protect him, Ishmael had to be sent away. Sarah was protecting the promised seed and heir.

21:9 The Hebrew verb translated laughing is ambiguous and may be interpreted as denoting either "mocking" or "playing." The verbal form used here possibly favors "mocking." Galatians 4:29 follows this interpretation. Ishmael was probably making fun of Isaac's role as Abraham's promised son.[13] However some Jewish resources have said that in the Hebrew the word 'playing" indicates sexual abuse[14] see end note) צָחַק

Gen 21:10 Wherefore she said unto Abraham, Cast out this bondwomen and her son: for the son of this

---

[13] Crossway Bibles. (2008). *The ESV Study Bible* (86). Wheaton, IL:

Crossway Bibles.

[14] †[צָחַק S⁶⁷¹¹ TWOT¹⁹⁰⁵ GK⁷⁴⁶⁴] **vb. laugh** (Arabic ضَحِكَ (*ḍaḥika*), *laugh*, Syriac ܓܚܟ (*ghek*), cf. Ba^ES 34; v. also שׂחק);—**Qal** *Pf.* 3 fs. צָחֲקָה Gn 18:13, etc.; *Impf.* 3 ms. יִצְחָק Gn 21:6, וַיִּצְחָק 17:17; 3 fs. וַתִּצְחַק 18:12;—*laugh*, Gn 18:12, 13, 15^(×2) (J), 17:17 (P); c. ל *at, concerning*, 21:6. **Pi.** *Impf.* וַיְצַחֵק Ju 16:25; *Inf. cstr.* לְצַחֶק Ex 32:6, (בְּי) צַחֵק בְּנוּ לְצַחֶק Gn 39:14, 17; *Pt.* מְצַחֵק Gn 19:14; 26:8, מְצַחֶק 21:9;— **1.** *jest* Gn 19:14 (J). **2.** *sport, play* Gn 21:9 (E); Ex 32:6 (J); *make sport* for Ju 16:25 (לְפְנֵי; || וַיִשַׂחֶק־לָנוּ); *toy with* (אֶת), of conjugal caresses Gn 26:8 (cf. Doughty^Arab. Des. i. 231), *make a toy of*, c. בְּ, 39:14, 17 (all J).[14]

bondwomen shall not be heir with my son, *even* with
Isaac.
Gen 21:11 And the thing was very grievous in
Abraham's sight because of his son.
Gen 21:12 And God said unto Abraham, Let it not be
grievous in thy sight because of the lad, and because of
thy bondwomen; in all that Sarah hath said unto thee,
hearken unto her voice; for in Isaac shall thy seed be
called. (KJV)

Sarah was a great role model and mother of Israel. When
she died all mourned her death. She was an example of
strength, godliness, purity and humility. The Midrash
states that all of Sarah's life was equally good.

Gen 23:1 And Sarah was an hundred and seven and
twenty years old: *these were* the years of the life of
Sarah.

Gen 23:2 And Sarah died in Kirjatharba; the same *is*
Hebron in the land of Canaan: and Abraham came to
mourn for Sarah, and to weep for her. (KJV)

And the life of Sarah was one hundred years and twenty
years and seven years: The reason that the word "years"
was written after every digit is to tell you that every digit
is to be expounded upon individually: when she was one
hundred years old, she was like a twenty-year-old
regarding sin. Just as a twenty-year-old has not sinned,
because she is not liable to punishment, so too when she
was one hundred years old, she was without sin. And

when she was twenty, she was like a seven-year-old as
regards to beauty. — from Gen. Rabbah 58:1]
the years of the life of Sarah: All of them equally good.

SARAI (Sĕr′ ī) Personal name meaning "princess." [iii][15]

In the Apostolic Scriptures Rom. 4:19 refers to Sarah's
barrenness as evidence of Abraham's faith;

Romans 4:19 And being not weak in faith, he
considered not his own body now dead, when he was
about an hundred years old, neither yet the deadness of
Sara's womb: (KJV)

Rom. 9:9 cites her conception of Isaac as an example of
God's power in fulfilling a promise.

Rom 9:9 For this *is* the word of promise, At this time will
I come, and Sara shall have a son. (KJV)

Galatians 4:21–31 contrasts her with Hagar without
naming her,

Gal 4:21 Tell me, ye that desire to be under the law, do
ye not hear the law?
Gal 4:22 For it is written, that Abraham had two sons,
the one by a bondmaid, the other by a freewomen.
Gal 4:23 But he *who was* of the bondwomen was born
after the flesh; but he of the freewomen *was* by promise.

---

[15] See end note regarding Sarah's name

Gal 4:24 Which things are an allegory: for these are the
two covenants; the one from the mount Sinai, which
gendereth to bondage, which is Agar.

Gal 4:25 For this Agar is mount Sinai in Arabia, and
answereth to Jerusalem which now is, and is in bondage
with her children.

Gal 4:26 But Jerusalem which is above is free, which is
the mother of us all.

Gal 4:27 For it is written, Rejoice, *thou* barren that
bearest not; break forth and cry, thou that travailest not:
for the desolate hath many more children than she which
hath an husband.

Gal 4:28 Now we, brethren, as Isaac was, are the
children of promise.

Gal 4:29 But as then he that was born after the flesh
persecuted him *that was born* after the Spirit, even so *it
is* now.

Gal 4:30 Nevertheless what saith the scripture? Cast out
the bondwomen and her son: for the son of the
bondwomen shall not be heir with the son of the
freewomen.

Gal 4:31 So then, brethren, we are not children of the
bondwomen, but of the free. (KJV)

Heb. 11:11 lauds her faith, and

Heb 11:11 Through faith also Sara herself received
strength to conceive seed, and was delivered of a child
when she was past age, because she judged him faithful
who had promised. (KJV)

1 Pet. 3:6 describes her relationship with Abraham.

1Pe 3:6 Even as Sara obeyed Abraham, calling him lord: whose daughters ye are, as long as ye do well, and are not afraid with any amazement. (KJV)

Sarah's obedience and faith had an impact on not only a nation called Israel but the world as well. She set the tone for all who would follow after her as an example of a woman, wife and mother. Even our Shabbat prayers make mention of her every Erev Shabbat with the following blessing over our daughters:

Y'sim–meikh elohim k'sara, rivka, rahell v'leah. May God, make you as Sarah, Rebecca, Rachel, & Leah.

Rebecca – Daughter of Israel with a Servants Heart

Rebecca's Profile in A Nutshell

Strengths and Accomplishments
- When confronted with a need, she took immediate action.
- She was accomplishment oriented.

- Weaknesses and Mistakes
- Her initiative was not always balanced with wisdom.
- She favored one of her sons.
- She deceived her husband.

Lessons from Her Life
- Our actions must be guided by God's Word.
- God makes use even of our mistakes in His plans.

Vital Statistics
- Where: Haran, Canaan
- Occupation: Wife, mother, household manager
- Relatives: Grandparents: Nahor and Milcah. Father: Bethuel.
- Husband: Isaac
- Brother: Laban
- Twin sons: Esau and Jacob

Lessons from Rebecca's Life

Little did Rebecca know that her day at the well was
going to change her life forever. Abraham instructs his
servant to find a wife for his son (Genesis 24:2)

Gen 24:2 And Abraham said unto his eldest servant of
his house, that ruled over all that he had, Put, I pray thee,
thy hand under my thigh:
Gen 24:3 And I will make thee swear by the LORD, the
God of heaven, and the God of the earth, that thou shalt
not take a wife unto my son of the daughters of the
Canaanites, among whom I dwell:
Gen 24:4 But thou shalt go unto my country, and to my
kindred, and take a wife unto my son Isaac.
Gen 24:5 And the servant said unto him, Peradventure
the women will not be willing to follow me unto this
land: must I needs bring thy son again unto the land from
whence thou camest?
Gen 24:6 And Abraham said unto him, Beware thou that
thou bring not my son thither again.
Gen 24:7 The LORD God of heaven, which took me
from my father's house, and from the land of my kindred,
and which spake unto me, and that sware unto me,
saying, Unto thy seed will I give this land; he shall send
his angel before thee, and thou shalt take a wife unto my
son from thence.
Gen 24:8 And if the women will not be willing to follow
thee, then thou shalt be clear from this my oath: only
bring not my son thither again.

Gen 24:9 And the servant put his hand under the thigh
of Abraham his master, and sware to him concerning that
matter. (KJV)

God already handpicked Rebecca to be Isaacs wife, even
though no one at the time knew how destiny would bring
these two-chosen people together to fulfill His plans and
purposes for a nation that was going to be a light to the
World that would eventually bring forth the Light of The
World Yeshua HaMashiach.

Avraham knew that not any women would do, it had to
be the one God choose from the foundations of the world
that would be the mother to Isaacs children. We see the
wisdom of Abraham's servant in the following verses.

Gen 24:10 And the servant took ten camels of the
camels of his master, and departed; for all the goods of
his master *were* in his hand: and he arose, and went to
Mesopotamia, unto the city of Nahor.
Gen 24:11 And he made his camels to kneel down
without the city by a well of water at the time of the
evening, *even* the time that women go out to draw *water.*
Gen 24:12 And he said, O LORD God of my master
Abraham, I pray thee, send me good speed this day, and
shew kindness unto my master Abraham.
Gen 24:13 Behold, I stand *here* by the well of water;
and the daughters of the men of the city come out to
draw water: (KJV)

Gen 24:14 And let it come to pass, that the damsel to
whom I shall say, Let down thy pitcher, I pray thee, that

I may drink; and she shall say, Drink, and I will give thy
camels drink also: *let the same be* she *that* thou hast
appointed for thy servant Isaac; and thereby shall I know
that thou hast shewed kindness unto my master. (KJV)

her have You designated: She is worthy of him, for she
will perform acts of kindness, and she is fit to enter the
house of Abraham; and the expression הֹכַחְתָּ means "You
chose," Rashi.

Gen 24:15 And it came to pass, before he had done
speaking, that, behold, Rebekah came out, who was born
to Bethuel, son of Milcah, the wife of Nahor, Abraham's
brother, with her pitcher upon her shoulder. (KJV)

Again, to Rebecca it was just another day at the well to
do her daily chores. Because she had a servant's heart,
she didn't give it a second thought about helping this
stranger or his camels as well.

**A look at the meaning of Rivka's name further
connects us to the concept of marriage:**

Rivka = "a yoke used to join two animals of the same
species together, to fulfill a purpose or work together in
the fields." (Hebrew-Hebrew dictionary, Even Shoshan)

Gen 24:16 And the damsel *was* very fair to look upon, a
virgin, neither had any man known her: and she went
down to the well, and filled her pitcher, and came up.
Gen 24:17 And the servant ran to meet her, and said, Let
me, I pray thee, drink a little water of thy pitcher.

Gen 24:18 And she said, Drink, my lord: and she hasted, and let down her pitcher upon her hand, and gave him drink.
Gen 24:19 And when she had done giving him drink, she said, I will draw *water* for thy camels also, until they have done drinking.
Gen 24:20 And she hasted, and emptied her pitcher into the trough, and ran again unto the well to draw *water,* and drew for all his camels.
Gen 24:21 And the man wondering at her held his peace, to wit whether the LORD had made his journey prosperous or not.
Gen 24:22 And it came to pass, as the camels had done drinking, that the man took a golden earring of half a shekel weight, and two bracelets for her hands of ten *shekels* weight of gold;
Gen 24:23 And said, Whose daughter *art* thou? tell me, I pray thee: is there room *in* thy father's house for us to lodge in?
Gen 24:24 And she said unto him, I *am* the daughter of Bethuel the son of Milcah, which she bare unto Nahor.
Gen 24:25 She said moreover unto him, We have both straw and provender enough, and room to lodge in.
Gen 24:26 And the man bowed down his head, and worshipped the LORD.
Gen 24:27 And he said, Blessed *be* the LORD God of my master Abraham, who hath not left destitute my master of his mercy and his truth: I *being* in the way, the LORD led me to the house of my master's brethren. (KJV)

In these verses, we see many of Rebecca's trait's
manifested.

#1. She was quick to take care of the stranger's needs.
#2. She went beyond what was asked and offered to take
care of the animals as well.
#3. She showed hospitality by inviting this stranger and
his animals to come to her home so they could have food
and lodging.

She was willing to go to a strange place because she was
sensitive to the voice of God and knew this was His will
for her.

Gen 24:58 And they called Rebekah, and said unto her,
Wilt thou go with this man? And she said, I will go.
(KJV)

**and she said, "I will go.": of my own accord, even if
you do not desire it. Rashi**

When Isaac sees her it is love at first sight!
Gen 24:63 And Isaac went out to meditate in the field at
the eventide: and he lifted up his eyes, and saw, and,
behold, the camels *were* coming.
Gen 24:64 And Rebekah lifted up her eyes, and when
she saw Isaac, she lighted off the camel. (KJV)

and saw Isaac: She saw his majestic appearance, and she
was astounded by him (Gen. Rabbah 60:14).
and she let herself down: She slipped off toward the
earth, as the Targum כִּינַת, "and she leaned." She leaned

towards the earth but did not reach the ground, as (above verse 14):"Please lower (הַטִּי) your pitcher," [which the Targum renders:] אַרְכִינִי [tilt]. Similar to this, (II Sam. 22:10):"And He bent (וַיֵּט) the heavens," [which the Targum renders:] וְאַרְכִין, an expression of leaning towards the earth, and similarly (Ps. 37: 24):"Though he falls (יִפֹּל), he will not be cast down," meaning that if he falls toward the earth, he will not reach the ground.

Gen 24:65 For she *had* said unto the servant, What man *is* this that walketh in the field to meet us? And the servant *had* said, It *is* my master: therefore she took a vail, and covered herself.
Gen 24:66 And the servant told Isaac all things that he had done.
Gen 24:67 And Isaac brought her into his mother Sarah's tent, and took Rebekah, and she became his wife; and he loved her: and Isaac was comforted after his mother's *death. (KJV)*

to the tent of Sarah his mother: He brought her to the tent, and behold, she was Sarah his mother; i.e., she became the likeness of Sarah his mother, for as long as Sarah was alive, a candle burned from one Sabbath eve to the next, a blessing was found in the dough, and a cloud was attached to the tent. When she died, these things ceased, and when Rebecca arrived, they resumed (Gen. Rabbah 60:16).

The Future Mother of 2 nations, but only 1 chosen.

Gen 25:20 And Isaac was forty years old when he took
Rebekah to wife, the daughter of Bethuel the Syrian of
Padanaram, the sister to Laban the Syrian.
Gen 25:21 And Isaac intreated the LORD for his wife,
because she *was* barren: and the LORD was intreated of
him, and Rebekah his wife conceived.
Gen 25:22 And the children struggled together within
her; and she said, If *it be* so, why *am* I thus? And she
went to enquire of the LORD.
Gen 25:23 And the LORD said unto her, Two nations
are in thy womb, and two manner of people shall be
separated from thy bowels; and *the one* people shall be
stronger than *the other* people; and the elder shall serve
the younger. (KJV)

Two nations are in your womb: [The word גוֹיִם] is written
גֵּיִים [which is pronounced] like גֵּאִים (exalted persons).
These were Antoninus and Rabbi [Judah the Prince],
from whose tables neither radishes nor lettuce were
lacking either in the summer or in the winter. — [From
Avodah Zarah 11a]
will separate from your innards: From the womb they are
separated, this one to his wickedness, and this one to his
innocence.
will become mightier than the other kingdom: They will
not be equal in greatness; when one rises, the other will
fall, and so [Scripture] states (Ezek. 26:2): "I shall
become full from the destroyed city." Tyre became full
[gained power] only from the destruction of Jerusalem.
— [From Meg. 6a, Pes. 42b]

Gen 25:24 And when her days to be delivered were
fulfilled, behold, *there were* twins in her womb. (KJV)

there were twins in her womb: [תוֹמִם is spelled]
defectively [missing an "aleph" and"yud"], but
concerning Tamar, it is written תְּאוֹמִים, with the plene
spelling, [with an "aleph" and"yud"] because they (Perez
and Zerah) were both righteous, but here, one was
righteous and one was wicked. — [From Gen. Rabbah
63:8]

Gen 25:25 And the first came out red, all over like an
hairy garment; and they called his name Esau.
Gen 25:26 And after that came his brother out, and his
hand took hold on Esau's heel; and his name was called
Jacob: and Isaac *was* threescore years old when she bare
them.
Gen 25:27 And the boys grew: and Esau was a cunning
hunter, a man of the field; and Jacob *was* a plain man,
dwelling in tents.
Gen 25:28 And Isaac loved Esau, because he did eat of
his venison: but Rebekah loved Jacob. (KJV)

*And said Hashem to her two nations are in your womb
and two peoples will separate from within you and to
one people will be fullness [and great] boldness and the
great will serve the junior."* Bereishis 25:22,23

Per Dr. Akiva Gamliel Belk[16]

*"There are interesting letters added to several of the
words in the first passuk. This is not by mistake. I have
noted these letters in red. The Yud represents the
intensity of the struggle between Ay Sawv {Eisov} and
Yaakov. The Tav in Vah Yeet Roh Tzah Tzoo represents
that this fighting in the womb of Rivkah was a sign. The
Tav in Vah Toh Mehr represents another sign. Rivkah
spoke out loud to her sons. "Why are you fighting?"
Like a mother would say to her children, "Why are you
fighting / hurting your brother?" Yet this was very
puzzeling to Rivkah.*

*Our sages state that when Rivkah would pass by the
doorways of Torah study at the school of Sheim and
Evier Yaakov would rush to come out, and when Rivkah
would pass by houses of idol worship Eisov would rush
to come out. Can you imagine how Rivkah must have
felt?*

*Let's examine this a little closer. Notice the phrase, Shih
Nay - Goh Yeem - Bih Veet Naych {Two nations are in
your womb} Within these three words there are two
unique acrostics.*

*The first acrostic is from the first letter of each of the
three words of the phrase Shih Nay - Goh Yeem - Bih
Veet Naych. The second acrostic follows the first as*

16

http://www.jewishpath.org/a_gematria/bereishis/might_subdued_by
_hatorah.html

*Yaakov followed Eisov in birth. This acrostic is taken
from the last letter of the last two words of the same
phrase."*

As a mother, she sensed that the children within her were
struggling for leadership as foretold by God before they
were born. She was entrusted with the duty to make sure
the one God choose would be the one to lead the future
nation of Israel.

She was spiritually sensitive to Gods plans and purposes
and knew that Jacob was to be the leader of God' s
people not Esau. She has been criticized for her actions,
even though they were deceptive, she saw God's greater
plans and purposes and knew that the blessings had to be
given to Jacob and not Esau. By doing this, she
preserved the righteous seed that would go forth and
bring forth the 12 Tribes of Israel.

Gen 27:5 And Rebekah heard when Isaac spake to Esau
his son. And Esau went to the field to hunt *for* venison,
and to bring *it.*
Gen 27:6 And Rebekah spake unto Jacob her son,
saying, Behold, I heard thy father speak unto Esau thy
brother, saying,
Gen 27:7 Bring me venison, and make me savoury
meat, that I may eat, and bless thee before the LORD
before my death.
Gen 27:8 Now therefore, my son, obey my voice
according to that which I command thee.

Gen 27:9 Go now to the flock, and fetch me from thence two good kids of the goats; and I will make them savoury meat for thy father, such as he loveth:

Gen 27:10 And thou shalt bring *it* to thy father, that he may eat, and that he may bless thee before his death.

Gen 27:11 And Jacob said to Rebekah his mother, Behold, Esau my brother *is* a hairy man, and I *am* a smooth man:

Gen 27:12 My father peradventure will feel me, and I shall seem to him as a deceiver; and I shall bring a curse upon me, and not a blessing.

Gen 27:13 And his mother said unto him, Upon me *be* thy curse, my son: only obey my voice, and go fetch me *them.*

Gen 27:14 And he went, and fetched, and brought *them* to his mother: and his mother made savoury meat, such as his father loved.

Gen 27:15 And Rebekah took goodly raiment of her eldest son Esau, which *were* with her in the house, and put them upon Jacob her younger son:

Gen 27:16 And she put the skins of the kids of the goats upon his hands, and upon the smooth of his neck:

Gen 27:17 And she gave the savoury meat and the bread, which she had prepared, into the hand of her son Jacob.

Gen 27:18 And he came unto his father, and said, My father: and he said, Here *am* I; who *art* thou, my son?

Gen 27:19 And Jacob said unto his father, I *am* Esau thy firstborn; I have done according as thou badest me: arise, I pray thee, sit and eat of my venison, that thy soul may bless me.

Gen 27:20 And Isaac said unto his son, How *is it* that
thou hast found *it* so quickly, my son? And he said,
Because the LORD thy God brought *it* to me.

Gen 27:21 And Isaac said unto Jacob, Come near, I pray
thee, that I may feel thee, my son, whether thou *be* my
very son Esau or not.

Gen 27:22 And Jacob went near unto Isaac his father;
and he felt him, and said, The voice *is* Jacob's voice, but
the hands *are* the hands of Esau.

Gen 27:23 And he discerned him not, because his hands
were hairy, as his brother Esau's hands: so he blessed
him.

Gen 27:24 And he said, *Art* thou my very son Esau?
And he said, I *am.*

Gen 27:25 And he said, Bring *it* near to me, and I will
eat of my son's venison, that my soul may bless thee.
And he brought *it* near to him, and he did eat: and he
brought him wine, and he drank.

Gen 27:26 And his father Isaac said unto him, Come
near now, and kiss me, my son.

Gen 27:27 And he came near, and kissed him: and he
smelled the smell of his raiment, and blessed him, and
said, See, the smell of my son *is* as the smell of a field
which the LORD hath blessed:

Gen 27:28 Therefore God give thee of the dew of
heaven, and the fatness of the earth, and plenty of corn
and wine:

Gen 27:29 Let people serve thee, and nations bow down
to thee: be lord over thy brethren, and let thy mother's
sons bow down to thee: cursed *be* every one that curseth
thee, and blessed *be* he that blesseth thee. (KJV)

We see that because of Rebecca's obedience and knowledge of God's will that the blessing was passed onto the rightful chosen leader of God's people, Jacob latter to be known as Israel! She had to make some tough decisions, going against the tradition of the blessing going to the older brother. She had to deceive her husband, who she greatly respected but knew that his favor towards Esau was not God's plan for His people. She loved both her sons, but recognized in Jacob the qualities of one who had what it would take to lead the people of Abraham. We will see how in Israel's future encounter with Esau that these events were all planned out by God and Rebecca was merely doing His will at the time. She was a woman of great wisdom and obedience with the heart of a servant.

Dina Coopersmith points out the following in her teaching on Rivkah[17]

"In Hebrew, the word for acts of kindness is "Gemilut Chesed" - literally: the weaning of kindness. (Gemilut means "to wean off.") Isn't this a contradiction in terms? Weaning means to distance oneself and create separation, while kindness means to give, connect and join.
We see from here that true kindness is to give the recipient the feeling that he is not receiving at all; rather that he is completely independent and weaned from you. Otherwise, the bit of shame that the recipient inevitably feels would make the kindness less complete.

---

[17]

http://www.aish.com/jl/b/women/Women_in_the_Bible_Rivka.html

This is the type of goodness which God bestows upon us: He gives us everything, but makes us think that we are working to arrange it and that we deserve it. (When in fact God is orchestrating everything!) This is the method we should emulate in marriage: We give to our partner, without giving the feeling that we are in charge and the benefactors.

This is Rivka's essence: From the time we first meet her, as she tirelessly and effortlessly draws water for man and beast, then in her marriage to Yitzhak and the birth of her sons, she influences them to do what she knows is best, but never at the expense of their self-respect.

How fitting, then, that Rivka appears for the first and then for the last time in the context of finding a marriage partner: the first time for Yitzhak, and the last time for Yaakov, her son. The quintessential matriarch of kindness, named for the double-yoke holding two disparate elements together, teaches us a lesson for eternity about weaning and independence, about marriage and the nature of real giving."

The Impact of Leah and Rachel and the Birthing of the 12 Tribes

A Tale of 2 Sisters – Genesis 28:1-30:25

Rachel –Beautiful, Loved, Barren (for a season), Birthed Joseph, Died giving birth to Benjamin

Rachel the very ancient word רחל (*rahel*), meaning ewe, occurs in several <u>Semitic</u> languages, all with the same meaning. We have no idea what the root of this word might be or what it may have meant.
Our word occurs four times in the Bible, in Genesis 31:8; Genesis 32:15; Song 6:6; and most famously in Isaiah 53:7, "Like a sheep — רחל (*rahel*) — that is silent before its shearers, so did He not open His mouth".[18]

Leah-Plain, Not Loved, Fruitful, Birthed 10 Tribes plus 1 daughter Dinah. The name Leah is identical to the verb לאה (*la'a*) meaning to be weary or grieved:

Leah -The verb לאה (*la'a*) means to be weary, grieved, offended (even impatient or slow says BDB Theological Dictionary). HAW Theological Wordbook of the Old Testament sums the meaning of this verb up as, "physical or psychological weariness". It may occur to someone who runs with footmen (Jeremiah 12:5), or folks who vainly try to find a way into a house (Genesis 19:11). It may happen when water has a disagreeable taste (Exodus 7:18) or when a person is so lazy that the mere effort of

---

[18] http://www.abarim-publications.com/Meaning/Rachel.html#.WFMDvPkrLIU

bringing food to his mouth wears him out (Proverbs 26:15).

This verb's sole derivation is the feminine noun תלאה (*tela'a*), toil, hardship (Exodus 18:8, Nehemiah 9:32).[19]

We see from the Scriptures that Jacob loved Rachel and wanted her in the first place. However, her brother Laban tricked Jacob and at the wedding made a switch giving him Leah instead. I always felt bad for Leah, she was given to a man who she knew didn't love her and I am sure felt rejection knowing that he was truly in love with her sister. Jacob loved Leah, but not in the way he loved and desired Rachel.

Gen 29:18 And Jacob loved Rachel; and he said: 'I will serve thee seven years for Rachel thy younger daughter.'
Gen 29:19 And Laban said: 'It is better that I give her to thee, than that I should give her to another man; abide with me.'
Gen 29:20 And Jacob served seven years for Rachel; and they seemed unto him but a few days, for the love he had to her.
Gen 29:21 And Jacob said unto Laban: 'Give me my wife, for my days are filled, that I may go in unto her.'
Gen 29:22 And Laban gathered together all the men of the place, and made a feast.
Gen 29:23 And it came to pass in the evening, that he took Leah his daughter, and brought her to him; and he went in unto her.

---

[19] http://www.abarim-publications.com/Meaning/Leah.html#.WFMESfkrLIU

Gen 29:24 And Laban gave Zilpah his handmaid unto
his daughter Leah for a handmaid.
Gen 29:25 And it came to pass in the morning that,
behold, it was Leah; and he said to Laban: 'What is this
thou hast done unto me? did not I serve with thee for
Rachel? wherefore then hast thou beguiled me?'
Gen 29:26 And Laban said: 'It is not so done in our
place, to give the younger before the first-born.
Gen 29:27 Fulfil the week of this one, and we will give
thee the other also for the service which thou shalt serve
with me yet seven other years.'
Gen 29:28 And Jacob did so, and fulfilled her week; and
he gave him Rachel his daughter to wife.
Gen 29:29 And Laban gave to Rachel his daughter
Bilhah his handmaid to be her handmaid.
Gen 29:30 And he went in also unto Rachel, and he
loved Rachel more than Leah, and served with him yet
seven other years (KJV)

It also must have been heartbreaking for Rachel as well
that on the day she was supposed to be wed to Jacob, her
sister is the bride instead! Not a good situation for either
of the sisters and I am sure there was a lot of tension as
well between them as we see in the following verses.

Gen 29:31 And the LORD saw that Leah was hated, and
he opened her womb; but Rachel was barren.
Gen 29:32 And Leah conceived, and bore a son, and she
called his name Reuben; for she said: 'Because the
LORD hath looked upon my affliction; for now my
husband will love me.'

Gen 29:33 And she conceived again, and bore a son; and said: 'Because the LORD hath heard that I am hated, He hath therefore given me this son also.' And she called his name Simeon.

Gen 29:34 And she conceived again, and bore a son; and said: 'Now this time will my husband be joined unto me, because I have borne him three sons.' Therefore was his name called Levi.

Gen 29:35 And she conceived again, and bore a son; and she said: 'This time will I praise the   LORD.' Therefore she called his name Judah; and she left off bearing.

Gen 30:1 And when Rachel saw that she bore Jacob no children, Rachel envied her sister; and she said unto Jacob: 'Give me children, or else I die.'

Gen 30:2 And Jacob's anger was kindled against Rachel; and he said: 'Am I in God's stead, who hath withheld from thee the fruit of the womb?'

Gen 30:3 And she said: 'Behold my maid Bilhah, go in unto her; that she may bear upon my knees, and I also may be builded up through her.'

Gen 30:4 And she gave him Bilhah her handmaid to wife; and Jacob went in unto her.

Gen 30:5 And Bilhah conceived, and bore Jacob a son.

Gen 30:6 And Rachel said: 'God hath judged me, and hath also heard my voice, and hath given me a son.' Therefore called she his name Dan.

Gen 30:7 And Bilhah Rachel's handmaid conceived again, and bore Jacob a second son.

Gen 30:8 And Rachel said: 'With mighty wrestlings have I wrestled with my sister, and have prevailed.' And she called his name Naphtali.

Gen 30:9 When Leah saw that she had left off bearing, she took Zilpah her handmaid, and gave her to Jacob to wife.

Gen 30:10 And Zilpah Leah's handmaid bore Jacob a son.

Gen 30:11 And Leah said: 'Fortune is come!' And she called his name Gad.

Gen 30:12 And Zilpah Leah's handmaid bore Jacob a second son.

Gen 30:13 And Leah said: 'Happy am I! for the daughters will call me happy.' And she called his name Asher.

Gen 30:14 And Reuben went in the days of wheat harvest, and found mandrakes in the field, and brought them unto his mother Leah. Then Rachel said to Leah: 'Give me, I pray thee, of thy son's mandrakes.'

Gen 30:15 And she said unto her: 'Is it a small matter that thou hast taken away my husband? and wouldest thou take away my son's mandrakes also?' And Rachel said: 'Therefore he shall lie with thee to-night for thy son's mandrakes.'

Gen 30:16 And Jacob came from the field in the evening, and Leah went out to meet him, and said: 'Thou must come in unto me; for I have surely hired thee with my son's mandrakes.' And he lay with her that night.

Gen 30:17 And God hearkened unto Leah, and she conceived, and bore Jacob a fifth son.

Gen 30:18 And Leah said: 'God hath given me my hire, because I gave my handmaid to my husband. And she called his name Issachar.

Gen 30:19 And Leah conceived again, and bore a sixth son to Jacob.

Gen 30:20 And Leah said: 'God hath endowed me with a good dowry; now will my husband dwell with me, because I have borne him six sons.' And she called his name Zebulun.
Gen 30:21 And afterwards she bore a daughter, and called her name Dinah.
Gen 30:22 And God remembered Rachel, and God hearkened to her, and opened her womb.
Gen 30:23 And she conceived, and bore a son, and said: 'God hath taken away my reproach.'
Gen 30:24 And she called his name Joseph, saying: 'The LORD add to me another son.' (JPS)

Gen 35:17 And it came to pass, when she was in hard labour, that the mid-wife said unto her: 'Fear not; for this also is a son for thee.'
Gen 35:18 And it came to pass, as her soul was in departing - for she died - that she called his name Ben-oni; but his father called him Benjamin.
Gen 35:19 And Rachel died, and was buried in the way to Ephrath - the same is Beth-lehem. (JPS Translation)

Leah is the mother of six of Jacob's sons, including his first four (Reuben, Simeon, Levi, and Judah), and later two more (Issachar and Zebulun), and a daughter (Dinah). According to the scriptures, God saw that Leah was "unloved" and opened her womb as consolation. Seeing that she is unable to conceive, Rachel offers her handmaid Bilhah to Jacob, and names and raises the two sons (Dan and Naphtali) that Bilhah bears. Leah responds by offering her handmaid Zilpah to Jacob, and names and raises the two sons (Gad and Asher) that

Zilpah bears. According to some commentaries, Bilhah
and Zilpah are actually half-sisters of Leah and Rachel.[20]

One day, Leah's firstborn son Reuben returns from the
field with mandrakes for his mother. Leah has not
conceived for a while, and this plant, whose roots
resemble the human body, is thought to be an aid to
fertility.[7] Frustrated that she is not able to conceive at
all, Rachel offers to trade her night with their husband in
return for the mandrakes. Leah agrees, and that night she
sleeps with Jacob and conceives Issachar. Afterwards she
gives birth to Zebulun and to a daughter, Dinah. After
that, God remembers Rachel and gives her two
sons, Joseph and Benjamin.[21]

Rabbi Tvi Freedman puts it this way "Rachel is the
embodiment of the *Shechinah* as She descends to care
for Her children, even to travel their journey of exile
with them. And so she ensures they will return.

Her sister, Leah, is also our mother, the *Shechinah*. Yet
she is the transcendent, concealed world; those hidden
things of the divine mind too deep for men to fathom.
She is the sphere of royalty, as She rises above to receive
in silent meditation.

Rachel is the world of revealed words and deeds. She
held beauty that Jacob could perceive and desire. But
Leah was too lofty, too far beyond all things, and so

---

[20] https://en.wikipedia.org/wiki/Leah#cite_note-loj-6
[21] https://en.wikipedia.org/wiki/Leah#cite_note-7

DAUGHTERS OF ISRAEL AND THEIR IMPACT IN GODS
KINGDOM PAST, PRESENT AND FUTURE

Jacob could not attach himself to her in the same way.
Yet it is from Leah that almost all of the Jewish nation
descends.[22]"

Chana Weisberg sums it up this way regarding the
rivalry of the sisters and their descendants as well "The
vast gulf dividing their respective worlds not only
affected their own lives, but continued as a rift in the
lives of their descendants.[23]

Beginning with the rivalry between Joseph (Rachel's
child) and his brothers (primarily Leah's children), who
sought to kill him but instead were placated by selling
him as a slave to a passing caravan—the schism keeps
resurfacing.

It was Moses, Leah's descendant, who redeemed our
people from their slavery in Egypt, but only Joshua—
Moses' disciple and Rachel's descendant—who was able
to lead the nation into the Holy Land.

---

[22] Rabbi Tzvi Freeman, a senior editor at Chabad.org, also
heads our Ask The Rabbi team. He is the author of Bringing
Heaven Down to Earth. To subscribe to regular updates of
Rabbi Freeman's writing, visit Freeman Files subscription.
FaceBook @RabbiTzviFreeman Periscope @Tzvi_Freeman
[23] Chana Weisberg is the editor of TheJewishWomen.org. She
lectures internationally on issues relating to women,
relationships, meaning, self-esteem and the Jewish soul. She
is the author of five popular books.

The rulership of our first national king,
King Saul (descendant of Rachel) was cut short by King
David (Leah's descendant), through whom a dynasty
would be established. But the schism again resurfaced
with the constant strife and divisiveness
between *malchut Yisrael* (the kingship of Israel)
and *malchut David* (the Davidic dynasty)."

Their impact, out of all the tribes of Israel from these
two sisters come two of the of the strongest of all the
Tribes, Judah and Joseph (Ephraim). From Joseph,
would become a type of Messiah Ben Yosef, the
suffering Servant (Yeshua Ben Yosef) the preserver of
Israel in Egypt. From Judah would come Messiah Ben
David (Yeshua Ben David, when he returns as King of
Kings and Lord of Lords).

The Impact of Deborah- Judge, Prophetess & Mother of Israel

The First Female General & Rabbi.

The only female judge, and also the only judge to be called a prophet, Deborah is a decisive figure in the defeat of the Canaanites, a victory told in two accounts, a prose narrative in Judges 4 and an ancient song known as the Song of Deborah, probably composed not long after the original events, possibly by Deborah herself, and preserved in Judges 5. In Judg 4:4, Deborah is identified as *eshet lappidot,* which may mean "woman of [the town] Lappidoth," "wife of [the man] Lappidoth," or "woman of torches" (that is, "fiery woman").[24]

Jdg 4:4 Now D'vorah, a woman and a prophet, the wife of Lapidot, was judging Isra'el at that time.
Jdg 4:5 She used to sit under D'vorah's Palm between Ramah and Beit-El, in the hills of Efrayim; and the people of Isra'el would come to her for judgment.
Jdg 4:6 She sent for Barak the son of Avino`am, from Kedesh in Naftali, and said to him: "Adonai has given you this order: 'Go, march to Mount Tavor, and take with you 10,000 men from the people of Naftali and Z'vulun.

---

[24] https://jwa.org/encyclopedia/article/deborah-bible **Tikva Frymer-Kensky** (1943–2006), a professor of Hebrew Bible and the History of Judaism in the Divinity School at the University of Chicago, also taught in the Law School and the Committees on the Ancient Mediterranean World and Jewish Studies. She held an M.A. and Ph.D. from Yale University.

Jdg 4:7 I will cause Sisra, the commander of Yavin's
army, to encounter you at the Kishon River with his
chariots and troops; and I will hand him over to you.' "
Jdg 4:8 Barak answered her: "If you go with me, I'll go;
but if you won't go with me, I won't go."
Jdg 4:9 She replied, "Yes, I will gladly go with you; but
the way you are doing it will bring you no glory; because
Adonai will hand Sisra over to a woman." Then D'vorah
set out and went with Barak to Kedesh. Complete
Jewish Bible

Strengths and Accomplishments:
- Fourth and only Female judge of Israel
- Special abilities as a mediator, advisor, and counselor.
- When called to lead, was able to plan, direct and delegate.
- Known for her prophetic power.
- A writer of songs.

Lessons from Her Life
- God chooses the leaders by his standards, not ours
- Wise leaders choose good helpers.

I must say that Deborah is one of my favorite Eishes
Chayel/Women of Valor. The only female judge
mentioned in the Book of Judges, she not only counsels
Israel on warfare, but also is a judge of Israel, which
means she was a Torah Scholar!

She not only was a wartime leader and Judge but a
Prophetess as well. She was a very gifted woman of
Elohim and her husband recognized the anointing upon
her as well. It takes strong man to submit to the
leadership of a woman, but a Godly man is one who
respects God's anointed whether they are Male or
Female and submits to the anointing of Elohim upon
them. My husband is such a man as this, he is my
backbone and sees the call and stands with me in the
call. We are one, we are a Team no matter who is the
mouthpiece, God gets the glory!

I believe she is a role model for many women who have
the call to ministry but who are not taken seriously when
it comes to teaching and leading.

From the Teacher's Commentary

"Deborah was one of these special women, who even
before the military victory over the Canaanites was
"judging" Israel from Ramah.

The term "judging" is important if we are to understand
this women's importance. A judge was more than a person
who settled disputes (which Deborah did: see 4:5). A
judge in Israel exercised all the functions of a governor:
he or she held executive and legislative authority, and
often military authority as well. We can sense Deborah's
authority as she "sends for" Barak, and he comes. It is
only when Barak arrives that Deborah speaks in her role

as prophetess, and tells him, "The Lord, the God of Israel, commands you."[25]"

Per Rosen "Biblical Women Unbound"[26]
JUDGES 4:4–10

Deborah, wife of Lappidoth, was a prophetess; she led Israel at that time. She used to sit under the Palm of Deborah, between Ramah and Bethel in the hill country of Ephraim, and the Israelites would come to her for decisions.

She summoned Barak son of Abinoam, of Kedesh in Naphtali, and said to him, "The Lord, the God of Israel, has commanded: Go, march up to Mount Tabor, and take with you ten thousand men of Naphtali and Zebulun. And I will draw Sisera, Jabin's army commander, with his chariots and his troops, toward you up to the Wadi Kishon; and I will deliver him into your hands." But Barak said to her, "If you will go with me, I will go; if not, I will not go." "Very well, I will go with you," she answered. "However, there will be no glory for you in the course you are taking, for then the Lord will deliver Sisera into the hands of a woman." So Deborah went with Barak to Kedesh. Barak then mustered Zebulun and Naphtali at Kedesh; ten thousand marched up after him; and Deborah also went up with him.

---

[25] Richards, L., & Richards, L. O. (1987). *The teacher's commentary* (183). Wheaton, IL: Victor Books.
[26] Rosen, N. (1996). *Biblical Women Unbound: Counter-Tales* (139–140). Philadelphia, PA: The Jewish Publication Society

COMMENTARY

Of all women in the Bible, Deborah seems least in need
of new midrash. Her text is heroic from first to last: she is
prophet, judge, general, and she sings her own victory
song.

She appears to have been dropped into the text from a very
great height. She exists not for marriage or childbirth,
belongs to no family narrative. Traditional midrash
questions very little about her and has little to impart. But
what is there is enough to suggest a drama of struggle
within the Bible story of triumph. Deborah, says midrash,
made mistakes. Instead of going to Barak, her husband,
she made him come to her, a sign of disrespect. The
midrash conclude that "eminence is not for women"
(Megillah, 146). They attribute to God the defense of their
own marital vulnerability, adding wishfully that Deborah
was punished by loss of prophetic power while she
composed the song that speaks too much of herself."[27]

I do not agree with the Midrash regarding Deborah being
disrespectful to her husband. She was simply fulfilling
the call that God has put upon her life and was respected
by all of Israel. Actions speak louder than words and she
was a woman of action both spiritually and naturally.
Sometimes the Midrash tends to read too much into the
text. If she was not an important leader in Israel because
she was a woman, then God would not have included
her. I believe he included her to encourage other women
who would follow in her footsteps as leaders as well as
Prophetess's.

---

[27] Rosen, N. (1996). *Biblical Women Unbound: Counter-Tales* (139–140).
Philadelphia, PA: The Jewish Publication Society.

The Word states she was a "Prophetess" and "Lead
Israel" as a Mother of Israel at the time.

4:1–5:31 Deborah. The fourth judge was Deborah (see
note on 4:4–5), whose story is the first extended account
in the book (cf. Gideon in chs. 6–8; Jephthah in ch. 11;
and Samson in chs. 13–16). While the pattern of
apostasy continues (esp. 4:1–3), Deborah distinguishes
herself as the godliest of all the judges; it is ironic that
the most distinguished judge was a woman (4:8–9). She
was a prophet (4:4) and "a mother in Israel" (5:7), and
many sought out her judicial decisions at the "palm of
Deborah" (4:5). She instructed Barak in the conduct of
the battle (4:9, 14) and led in the victory song in ch. 5,
where she figures prominently (5:7, 12, 15). Deborah's
actions and words consistently pointed to God, not away
from him, in contrast to the poor choices of judges like
Gideon, Jephthah, and Samson.[28]

4:4–5 Deborah is called a prophetess, one of five such
women in the OT (cf. Miriam [Ex. 15:20]; Huldah [2
Kings 22:14]; Isaiah's wife [Isa. 8:3]; and Noadiah [a
false prophetess; Neh. 6:14]). Deborah functioned as a
civil leader (Judg. 4:6–10; 5:7) and as a judge who
decided cases (4:4–5). She lived in southern Ephraim,
near Judah.

4:6–9 Has not the LORD, the God of Israel, commanded
you? Deborah did not lead the army herself, but

---

[28] Crossway Bibles. (2008). *The ESV Study Bible* (444–445). Wheaton, IL:
Crossway Bibles.

challenged Barak, a man, to do so (see also v. 14); a
woman would not normally be a military leader in Israel.
In response, Barak summoned the tribes of Israel and led
the army (see vv. 10, 14, 15, 16, 22). At least six tribes
participated in the battle: Naphtali and Zebulun (v. 6),
Ephraim, Benjamin, Manasseh (Machir), and Issachar
(5:14–15). This is the nearest thing to an "all-Israelite"
coalition in the book. To his discredit, Barak hesitated to
lead the Israelites in battle (4:8). Thus, Deborah agreed
to go with him but predicted that the glory for the battle
would go to a woman (see note on 5:24–27).[29]

It takes a strong spiritual woman to take on the role that
Deborah took on. In fact, besides Esther, she is one of
the few women in the Tenach honored by being
mentioned in the Holy Book.

As a Female Rabbi myself, I know what it is like to live
with the ever present criticism of being a leader. I even
had a man email me telling me that I need to change the
name of my ministry and shut up! I am in no way a
woman's Liber, I detest that, my only desire is to please
the one who called me no matter how hot the water
might get! I am also grateful to the many men in
leadership who have recognized the call upon my life
and have treated me as a spiritual equal. Unfortunately,
the many "Deborah's" out there are very seldom given
the same respect in ministry as the "Barak's" are. But in
the long run it does not matter what man may say, it only
matters that we strive to be the Women of God that He

---

[29] Crossway Bibles. (2008). *The ESV Study Bible* (445). Wheaton, IL:
Crossway Bibles.

has called us to be and live a life that will not bring a
reproach upon His name.

As we begin our Study about D'Vorah, here are what
some of the Bible Commentaries say about her.[30]

DEBORAH/D'VORAH (Dehb' aw rah) Personal name
meaning, "bee." Deborah is the name of two women in
the Bible, Rebekah's nurse (Gen. 35:8; 24:59) and a
leader of pre-monarchic Israel (Judg. 4-5).

2. Deborah, the leader of Israel, is identified as a
prophetess, a judge, and the wife of Lapidoth (Judg.
4:4). She probably lived about 1200 B.C. or slightly later
during a period of Canaanite oppression. Deborah is
described in Judg. 5:7 as "a mother in Israel" because of
her role in delivering God's people. After Moses, only
Samuel filled the same combination of offices: prophet,
judge, and military leader.

Deborah served regularly as a judge, hearing and
deciding cases brought to her by the people of Israel. She
held court at "the palm tree of Deborah," in the southern
part of the territory of Ephraim, between Ramah and
Bethel (Judg. 4:4-5). Nothing is said about the
procedures at her court or about the extent of her
jurisdiction.

---

[30] Crossway Bibles. (2008). *The ESV Study Bible* (444–445). Wheaton, IL:
Crossway Bibles.

As a prophet, Deborah summoned Barak and
delivered an oracle giving him God's instructions for a
battle in the Jezreel Valley against the Canaanite army
commanded by Sisera (Judg. 4:6-9; compare Samuel in 1
Sam. 15:2-3 and the unnamed prophet in 1 Kings 20:13-
15). Barak obeyed, and the Israelites won the battle.
Some scholars believe that Deborah as prophet also
composed the victory poem she and Barak sang in
Judges 5. Deborah's authority under God was evidenced
by Barak's desire to have her present with him in the
army camp (Judg. 4:8,14) and by the testimony to her
leadership in the song (Judg. 5:7,12,15).

Tamara Kadari Deborah As A Prophet[31]   Deborah is
included among the seven women prophets of Israel
enumerated by the Rabbis: Sarah, Miriam,
Deborah, Hannah,
Abigail, Huldah and Esther (BT *Megillah* loc. cit.).
The midrash asks why Deborah had to judge Israel and
prophesy to them in a generation when the High Priest
Phinehas ben Eleazar was still alive. Rather, a person's
deeds dictate whether he merits attaining the spirit of
divine inspiration, whether Gentile or Israelite, whether
man or woman, and even if a slave or handmaiden.
Deborah was granted wisdom and prophecy because of

---

[31] **Tamar Kadari** received a B.A. in Hebrew Literature and an M.A. and
Ph.D. in Midrash at the Hebrew University of Jerusalem. She teaches
Midrash at Bar Ilan University and at the Schechter Institute of Jewish
Studies. During her period as a doctoral candidate she was a fellow at the
Center for Judaic Studies at the University of Pennsylvania. Her academic
research focuses on *Song of Songs Rabbah* and its early interpretations.

her deeds, the preparation of thick wicks for the
Tabernacle (see above, "Wife of Lappidoth"). Deborah
"was a prophet […] She used to sit […] between Ramah
and Bethel" (Jud. 4:4–5); and of Samuel it is said (I Sam.
7:17): "Then he would return to Ramah, for his home
was there, and there too he would judge Israel." In this
manner God rewarded Deborah for her good deeds. Just
as Samuel was at "Ramah," so, too, was Deborah at
"Ramah" (_Seder Eliyahu Rabbah_, Chap. 10, 48–50).
This exegesis interprets "Ramah" (literally, height) as
descriptive of the spiritual qualities of the prophecy of
Deborah and of Samuel, in order to compare Deborah's
prophetic ability with that of Samuel, the great prophet.

According to the Middrash below prophecy departed
Deborah because of her pride. However, I do not see this
indicated anywhere in scripture. We need to remember
that midrash is not scripture, but an interpretation or
story. In Judaism, the **Midrash** is the body of exegesis of
Torah texts along with homiletic stories as taught by
Chazal (Rabbinical Jewish sages of the post-Temple era)
that provide an intrinsic analysis to passages in the
Tanakh I do not agree with this particular midrash
regarding Deborah, because scripture indicates just the
opposite and gives her honor by including her in the
Word of God.

In the midrashic account, prophecy departed from
Deborah because of her pride. The Talmud declares that
when a person becomes haughty, if he was a sage, his
wisdom departs from him; and if a prophet, his ability to
prophesy departs from him. The Rabbis learn of this loss
of prophecy from Deborah, who boasted (Jud. 5:7):
"Deliverance ceased, ceased in Israel, till you arose, O
Deborah, arose, O mother, in Israel!" (In this verse
Deborah portrays the helplessness of Israel that
continued until she arose and delivered Israel.) In the
midrashic reading, prophecy departed from her as
punishment for her arrogance, leading her to plead (v.
12): "Awake, awake, O Deborah! Awake, awake,
[Deborah,] strike up the [prophetic] chant!" In these
words Deborah requests that the prophetic spirit return to
her (BT *Pesahim* 66b). According to another tradition
her haughtiness expresses itself by the fact that she sent
someone to call for Barak (Jud. 10:4) and did not go
herself. The Gemara comments that haughtiness is not
becoming for women. Deborah and Huldah are guilty of
the sin of pride and consequently both of them received
ugly names: Ziburta (bee) and Karkushta (rat)
(BT *Megillah* 14b). These midrashim might possibly
evince a certain degree of Rabbinic displeasure with the
character of Deborah as reflected in the Biblical

narrative, and with the upsetting of the accepted balance of power between the sexes.[32]

The primary attribute of a prophet in the Jewish tradition is to serve as a channel of communication between the human and YHWH.

Jdg 4:4 - And Deborah, a prophetess, the wife of Lapidoth,.... Deborah was a name common to women with the eastern people, see Gen 35:8; as Melissa, which is of the same signification with the Greeks, and both signify a "bee"; and to which Deborah answered in her industry, sagacity, and sweetness of temper to her friends, and sharpness to her enemies: she was a "prophetess", and foretold things to come, as the drawing of Sisera and his army to a certain place named by her, the victory that should be gained over him, and the delivery of him into the hands of a woman. Who Lapidoth was, or what is meant by the name, is not certain; most take it to be the name of her husband, which seems best, but who he was is not known; the Jews will have him to be the same with Barak, there being, as they think, some agreement in the names, Barak signifying lightning, and Lapidoth, lamps; but the whole context shows the contrary, that he was not her husband. Some render the words, "a woman of

---

[32] **Tamar Kadari** received a B.A. in Hebrew Literature and an M.A. and Ph.D. in Midrash at the Hebrew University of Jerusalem. She teaches Midrash at Bar Ilan University and at the Schechter Institute of Jewish Studies. During her period as a doctoral candidate she was a fellow at the Center for Judaic Studies at the University of Pennsylvania. Her academic research focuses on *Song of Songs Rabbah* and its early interpretations.

Lapidoth", taking it for the name of her native place on habitation; but where there was a place of this name no account can be given: some say she was so called from her employment before she was a prophetess and judge, making wicks for the lamps in the sanctuary, as Jarchi relates; and others take it to be expressive of her excellencies and virtues, which shone in her as lamps; the first sense is best:

she judged Israel at that time; toward the close of the twenty years' oppression under Jabin, being raised up of God as other judges were, and eminently endowed with gifts and grace; she endeavored to convince the people of their sins, exhorted them to repentance, and was a means of reforming them, and administering justice and judgment in all cases brought before her; and which Jabin might admit of, connive at, or take no notice of, she being a woman, of whose growing power and interest he had no jealousy.

Jdg 4:4 - And Deborah, a prophetess--A woman of extraordinary knowledge, wisdom, and piety, instructed in divine knowledge by the Spirit and accustomed to interpret His will; who acquired an extensive influence, and was held in universal respect, insomuch that she became the animating spirit of the government and discharged all the special duties of a judge, except that of military leader.

the wife of Lapidoth--rendered by some, "a woman of splendors."

Jdg 4:4-5 -
At that time the Israelites were judged by *Deborah*, a prophetess, the wife of Lapidoth, who dwelt under the Deborah-palm between Ramah (er Râm: see at Jos_18:25) and Bethel (Beitin: see atJos_7:2) in the tribe of Benjamin, upon the mountains of Ephraim. Deborah is called אשה נמיאה on account of her prophetic gift, like Miriam in Exo_15:20, and Hulda the wife of Shallum in 2Ki_22:14. This gift qualified her to judge the nation (the participle שפטה expresses the permanence of the act of judging), i.e., first of all to settle such disputes among the people themselves as the lower courts were unable to decide, and which ought therefore, according to Deu_17:8, to be referred to the supreme judge of the whole nation. The palm where she sat in judgment (cf. Psa_9:5) was called after her the *Deborah*-palm. The Israelites went up to her there to obtain justice. The expression *"came up"* is applied here, as in Deu_17:8, to the place of justice, as a spiritual height, independently of the fact that the place referred to here really stood upon an eminence.[33]
Deborah; associated with Barak in Judging Israel

Jdg 4:4 Now Devorah, a prophetess the wife of Lappidot, she judged Yisra'el at that time. (CJB)

---

[33] Crossway Bibles. (2008). *The ESV Study Bible* (444–445). Wheaton, IL: Crossway Bibles

Here are some other references to women who were
prophetesses in the Bible and that YHWH anointed for
that purpose. He will anoint who He wants to anoint
whether they are male or female. The office of a Prophet
is one of the fivefold ministry gifts.

Eph 4:10 He who descended is the one who also
ascended far above all the heavens, that he might fill all
things.
Eph 4:11 He gave some to be emissaries; and some,
prophets; and some, evangelists; and some, shepherds
and teachers;
Eph 4:12 for the perfecting of the holy ones, to the work
of serving, to the building up of the body of Messiah;
(CJB)

It is also part of the Gifts of the Ruach HaKodesh to the
Body of Messiah

1Co 12:5 There are various kinds of service, and the
same Lord.
1Co 12:6 There are various kinds of workings, but the
same God, who works all things in all.
1Co 12:7 But to each one is given the manifestation of
the Spirit for the profit of all.
1Co 12:8 For to one is given through the Spirit the word
of wisdom, and to another the word of knowledge,
according to the same Spirit;
1Co 12:9 to another faith, by the same Spirit; and to
another gifts of healings, by the same Spirit;
1Co 12:10 and to another workings of miracles; and to
another prophesy; and to another discerning of spirits; to

another different kinds of languages; and to another the
interpretation of languages.
1Co 12:11 But the one and the same Spirit works all of
these, distributing to each one separately as he desires.
(TLV)

PROPH'ETESS, n. A female prophet; a woman who
foretells future events, as Miriam, Huldah, Anna, &c.
Exo 15. Judg 4. Lk 2.

H5031 –Strongs - Prophetess
נביאה
n^ebîy'âh
neb-ee-yaw'
Feminine of H5030; a *prophetess* or
(generally) *inspired* women; by implication a *poetess*; by
association a *prophet's wife:* - prophetess.

H5031-Brown-Driver-Briggs Hebrew definitions
נביאה
nebîy'âh
BDB Definition:
1) prophetess
1a) ancient type endowed with gift of song (Miriam)
1b) later type consulted for a word (Huldah)
1c) false prophetess (Noadiah)
1d) wife of Isaiah the prophet
Part of Speech: noun feminine
A Related Word by BDB/Strong's Number: from H5030
Same Word by TWOT Number: 1277c

Act 21:8 On the next day, we, who were Sha'ul's
companions, departed, and came to Caesarea. We entered
into the house of Philip the evangelist, who was one of
the seven, and stayed with him.
Act 21:9 Now this man had four virgin daughters who
prophesied.(CJB)

1Co 11:4 Every man praying or prophesying, having his
head covered, dishonors his head.
1Co 11:5 But every women praying or prophesying with
her head unveiled dishonors her head. For it is one and
the same thing as if she were shaved. (CJB)

G4395 – Greek Strongs Prophesying
προφητεύω
prophēteuō
prof-ate-yoo'-o
From G4396;
to *foretell* events, *divine*, *speak* under *inspiration*, *exercis
e* the prophetic *office:* - prophesy.

It does not say – Women cannot prophesy; it says their
head should be covered when they do.

Gal 3:27 For as many of you as were immersed into
Messiah have put on Messiah.
Gal 3:28 There is neither Jew nor Greek, there is neither
slave nor free man, there is neither male nor female; for
you are all one in Messiah Yeshua.
Gal 3:29 If you are Messiah's, then you are Avraham's
seed and heirs according to promise.(CJB)

The Story of Deborah/D'vorah – She simply did what
YHWH anointed her to do and Barak and other leaders
recognized that anointing upon her.

Jdg 4:1 The children of Yisra'el again did that which
was evil in the sight of the LORD, when Ehud was dead.
Jdg 4:2 The LORD sold them into the hand of Yavin
king of Kena`an, who reigned in Chatzor; the captain of
whose army was Sisera, who lived in Charoshet of the
Gentiles.
Jdg 4:3 The children of Yisra'el cried to the LORD: for
he had nine hundred chariots of iron; and twenty years
he mightily oppressed the children of Yisra'el. (CJB)

A judge and prophetess

Jdg 4:4 Now Devorah, a prophetess, the wife of
Lappidot, she judged Yisra'el at that time.
Jdg 4:5 She lived under the palm tree of Devorah
between Ramah and Beit-El in the hill country of
Efrayim: and the children of Yisra'el came up to her for
judgment. (CJB
Deborah - H1683 – Strongs
דְּבוֹרָה / דְּברה
debôrâh / debôrâh
BDB Definition:
Deborah = "bee"

Deborah Summons Barak to deliver Israel

Jdg 4:6 She sent and called Barak the son of Avino`am
out of Kedesh-Naftali, and said to him, Hasn't the

LORD, the God of Yisra'el, commanded, [saying], Go
and draw to Mount Tavor, and take with you ten
thousand men of the children of Naftali and of the
children of Zevulun?

Barak - H1301
בָּרָק
bârâq
BDB Definition:
Barak = "lightning" or "lightning flash"

Jdg 4:7 I will draw to you, to the river Kishon, Sisera,
the captain of Yavin's army, with his chariots and his
multitude; and I will deliver him into your hand.
Jdg 4:8 Barak said to her, If you will go with me, then I
will go; but if you will not go with me, I will not go.

Deborah Agrees to accompany him to battle

Jdg 4:9 She said, I will surely go with you:
notwithstanding, the journey that you take shall not be
for your honor; for the LORD will sell Sisera into the
hand of a woman. Devorah arose, and went with Barak
to Kedesh.
Jdg 4:10 Barak called Zevulun and Naftali together to
Kedesh; and there went up ten thousand men at his feet:
and Devorah went up with him.
Jdg 4:11 Now Chever the Keni had separated himself
from the Kinim, even from the children of Chovav the
brother-in-law of Moshe, and had pitched his tent as far
as the oak in Tza`anannim, which is by Kedesh.

Jdg 4:12 They told Sisera that Barak the son of
Avino`am was gone up to Mount Tavor.
Jdg 4:13 Sisera gathered together all his chariots, even
nine hundred chariots of iron, and all the people who
were with him, from Charoshet of the Gentiles, to the
river Kishon.
Inspires him to action. (CJB)

Jdg 4:14 Devorah said to Barak, Up; for this is the day
in which the LORD has delivered Sisera into your hand;
hasn't the LORD gone out before you? So Barak went
down from Mount Tavor, and ten thousand men after
him.
Jdg 4:15 The LORD confused Sisera, and all his
chariots, and all his army, with the edge of the sword
before Barak; and Sisera alighted from his chariot, and
fled away on his feet.
Jdg 4:16 But Barak pursued after the chariots, and after
the army, to Charoshet of the Gentiles: and all the army
of Sisera fell by the edge of the sword; there was not a
man left.
Jdg 4:17 However Sisera fled away on his feet to the
tent of Ya`el the wife of Chever the Keni; for there was
shalom between Yavin the king of Chatzor and the house
of Chever the Keni.
Jdg 4:18 Ya`el went out to meet Sisera, and said to him,
Turn in, my lord, turn in to me; don't be afraid. He came
in to her into the tent, and she covered him with a rug.
Jdg 4:19 He said to her, Please give me a little water to
drink; for I am thirsty. She opened a bottle of milk, and
gave him drink, and covered him.

Jdg 4:20 He said to her, Stand in the door of the tent, and it shall be, when any man does come and inquire of you, and say, Is there any man here? that you shall say, No.

Jdg 4:21 Then Ya`el Chever's wife took a tent peg, and took a hammer in her hand, and went softly to him, and struck the pin into his temples, and it pierced through into the ground; for he was in a deep sleep; so he swooned and died.

Jdg 4:22 Behold, as Barak pursued Sisera, Ya`el came out to meet him, and said to him, Come, and I will show you the man whom you seek. He came to her; and behold, Sisera lay dead, and the tent peg was in his temples.

Jdg 4:23 So God subdued on that day Yavin the king of Kena`an before the children of Yisra'el.

Jdg 4:24 The hand of the children of Yisra'el prevailed more and more against Yavin the king of Kena`an, until they had destroyed Yavin king of Kena`an. (CJB)

Sings a Song of victory – vs 1-31

Jdg 5:1 Then Devorah and Barak the son of Avino`am sang on that day, saying,

Jdg 5:2 Because the leaders took the lead in Yisra'el, because the people offered themselves willingly, be blessed, the LORD! (CJB)

Victory came BECAUSE:

1. Because the leaders took the lead in Israel
2. Because the people offered themselves willingly

Jdg 5:3 Hear, you kings! Give ear, you princes! I, [even]
I, will sing to the LORD. I will sing praise to the LORD,
the God of Yisra'el.
Jdg 5:4 LORD, when you went forth out of Se`ir, when
you marched out of the field of Edom, the earth
trembled, the sky also dropped. Yes, the clouds dropped
water.
Jdg 5:5 The mountains quaked at the presence of the
LORD, even Sinai, at the presence of the LORD, the
God of Yisra'el.
Jdg 5:6 In the days of Shamgar the son of `Anat, in the
days of Ya`el, the highways were unoccupied. The
travelers walked through byways.
Jdg 5:7 The rulers ceased in Yisra'el. They ceased until
I, Devorah, arose; Until I arose a mother in Yisra'el.
(CJB)

Rulers ceased ruling in Israel, until Devorah arose and
was willing to walk in the anointing YHWH place upon
her life in humility and submission to Divine order.

Jdg 5:8 They chose new gods. Then war was in the
gates. Was there a shield or spear seen among forty
thousand in Yisra'el?
Jdg 5:9 My heart is toward the governors of Yisra'el,
who offered themselves willingly among the people.
Bless the LORD! (CJB)

Again – Willing hearts arose among the people to do
YHWH's will

Jdg 5:10 Tell [of it], you who ride on white donkeys, you who sit on rich carpets, and you who walk by the way.

Jdg 5:11 Far from the noise of archers, in the places of drawing water, there they will rehearse the righteous acts of the LORD, [Even] the righteous acts of his rule in Yisra'el. Then the people of the LORD went down to the gates.

Jdg 5:12 Awake, awake, Devorah! Awake, awake, utter a song! Arise, Barak, and lead away your captives, you son of Avino`am.

Jdg 5:13 Then a remnant of the nobles [and] the people came down. The LORD came down for me against the mighty.

Jdg 5:14 Those whose root is in `Amalek came out of Efrayim, after you, Binyamin, among your peoples. Governors come down out of Makhir. Those who handle the marshal's staff came out of Zevulun.

Jdg 5:15 The princes of Yissakhar were with Devorah. As was Yissakhar, so was Barak. They rushed into the valley at his feet. By the watercourses of Re'uven, there were great resolves of heart. (CJB)

The princes of Issachar were with D'vorah – The tribe of Issachar were the Torah Scholars in Israel, when in the wilderness, they were camped with Judah and Zebulun. They were known as the Tribe of Torah. (Numbers 2:3-5) They were known for setting up Torah Tents (Schools) in Israel.

even Issachar: not the princes only, but the whole tribe also; so the Targum paraphrases it, "the rest of the tribe

of Issachar:" as Issachar, so Barak; he was sent, &c. the
one as the other, with equal readiness and cheerfulness,
courage and intrepidity, descended the mountain, at the
order of Deborah, and took the field in the open plain, to
engage with Sisera and his numerous host:

Genesis 49:14 – "Yissaker is a strong donkey lying
between two burdens. And he saw that a resting place ws
good and that the land was pleasant and he inclined his
shoulder to bear a burden and become a subject to slave
labor. "Moshe Rabainu; Duet 33:18 "To your tents"
Also; 1 Chronicles 12:32 "And of the children of
Issachar, men that had understanding of the times, to
know what Israel ought to do , the heads of them were
two hundred; and all their brethren were at their
commandment' (Rashi)

There was great resolve in their hearts – They were
determined to see victory.

She rebukes the indifference of the tribes

Jdg 5:16 Why did you sit among the sheepfolds, To hear
the whistling for the flocks? At the watercourses of
Re'uven There were great searching's of heart.
Jdg 5:17 Gil`ad lived beyond the Yarden. Why did Dan
remain in ships? Asher sat still at the haven of the sea,
and lived by his creeks.
Jdg 5:18 Zevulun was a people that jeopardized their
lives to the deaths; Naftali also, on the high places of the
field. (CJB)

Jdg 5:19 The kings came and fought, then the kings of
Kena`an fought at Ta`nakh by the waters of Megiddo.
They took no plunder of silver.
Jdg 5:20 From the sky the stars fought. From their
courses, they fought against Sisera.
Jdg 5:21 The river Kishon swept them away, that
ancient river, the river Kishon. My soul, march on with
strength.
Jdg 5:22 Then the horse hoofs stamped because of the
prancings, the prancings of their strong ones.
Jdg 5:23 Curse Meroz, said the angel of the LORD.
Curse bitterly its inhabitants, because they didn't come to
help the LORD, to help the LORD against the mighty.
(CJB)

Jdg 5:24 Ya`el shall be blessed above women, the wife
of Chever the Keni; blessed shall she be above women in
the tent. (CJB)

Under Deborah's leadership the land of Israel had rest –
peace for 40 years.

Here is what Dr. Holisa Alewine of Israelnet.TV says of
Deborah/D'Vorah from an article she wrote on "Women
in Ministry"[34]

"The first Tanakh picture of a woman anointed as a judge
and military leader is contained in Judges 4:4-5:31.
D'vorah is raised up to be a hero in Israel among the

---

[34] Dr Holisa Alewine – Author and Lecturer on the Hebrew Roots Network
and author of The Creation Gospels

likes of judges such as Gideon, Sampson and Joshua. To
view her according to the pattern, we see her in
Scriptures in this order; a wife, a judge over Israel, a co-
commander of Israel's army. Once her marriage
relationship to Lappidot is established, the next role is
that of a judge over Israel, a role corresponding to an
elder. In order to judge, D'vorah must have studied,
applied, lived and taught Torah, for no judge is to apply
Adonai's rulings in judgment without a thorough
knowledge of Torah. Since there is no mention of
corruption during her tenure, we cannot assume that she
is one of the many unrighteous judges of that epoch who
applied the Torah with partiality. Also noted is that she
was sought after for her judgments, so the Israelites must
have been willing to accept her authority and Torah
scholarship regardless of any cultural norms.

Men and women are created to function in spiritual
submission to one another, fulfilling the purposes of
YHVH in unity. D'Vorah submits the leadership of the
physical battle to Barak, Barak in turn submits to
D'vorah's tactical instructions and leadership gift
endowed by YHWH. We can learn from her wisdom in
handling the issue of gender that women should be
sensitive to community perception of her roles. Her
response to her anointing is not arrogance or an attempt
to domineer over Barak, but willingness to share the
mission and its blessings according to the Edenic
pattern. Although sensitive to cultural norms, she does
not, however, refuse the mission because of gender
issues. She recognizes God's calling as higher than that
of her cultural role. In this example of a man and women

answering the higher call, we have an excellent Biblical picture of the example we should follow; a woman submitted to her husband or male covering, allowed and encouraged to operate in her anointing. There is mutual submission, just as Paul encouraged husbands and wives to do. [35]

---

[35] Dr Holisa Alewine – Author and Lecturer on the Hebrew Roots Network and author of The Creation Gospels

The Impact of Jael who arose during this battle and is called "Blessed above Women"

Jdg 4:18 Ya`el went out to meet Sisera, and said to him, Turn in, my lord, turn in to me; don't be afraid. He came in to her into the tent, and she covered him with a rug.
Jdg 4:19 He said to her, Please give me a little water to drink; for I am thirsty. She opened a bottle of milk, and gave him drink, and covered him.
Jdg 4:20 He said to her, Stand in the door of the tent, and it shall be, when any man does come and inquire of you, and say, Is there any man here? that you shall say, No.
Jdg 4:21 Then Ya`el Chever's wife took a tent peg, and took a hammer in her hand, and went softly to him, and struck the pin into his temples, and it pierced through into the ground; for he was in a deep sleep; so he swooned and died.
Jdg 4:22 Behold, as Barak pursued Sisera, Ya`el came out to meet him, and said to him, Come, and I will show you the man whom you seek. He came to her; and behold, Sisera lay dead, and the tent peg was in his temples.
Jdg 4:23 So God subdued on that day Yavin the king of Kena`an before the children of Yisra'el.
Jdg 4:24 The hand of the children of Yisra'el prevailed more and more against Yavin the king of Kena`an, until they had destroyed Yavin king of Kena`an. (CJB)

The Word Blessed in Hebrew is Barak

H1288 – Strongs - Blessed

בָּרַךְ

bârak

BDB Definition:

1) to bless, kneel

1a) (Qal)

1a1) to kneel

1a2) to bless

1b) (Niphal) to be blessed, bless oneself

1c) (Piel) to bless

1d) (Pual) to be blessed, be adored

1e) (Hiphil) to cause to kneel

1f) (Hithpael) to bless oneself

2) (TWOT) to praise, salute, curse

Part of Speech: verb

A Related Word by BDB/Strong's Number: a primitive root

Same Word by TWOT Number: 285

Jdg 5:24 [36]

Jael behaved altogether differently, although she was not an Israelite, but a woman of the tribe of the Kenites, which was only allied with Israel
(see Jdg_4:11, Jdg_4:17.). For her heroic deed she was to be blessed before women (מִן as in Gen_3:14, literally removed away from women). The *"women in the tent"* are dwellers in tents, or shepherdesses. This heroic act is

---

[36] From "Women in the Bible Books"

poetically commemorated in the strophe which follows
inJdg_5:25-27.

What Jael did[37]

Jdg 5:25 He asked for water. She gave him milk. She
brought him butter in a lordly dish.
Jdg 5:26 She put her hand to the tent peg, and her right
hand to the workmen's hammer. With the hammer she
struck Sisera. She struck through his head. Yes, she
pierced and struck through his temples.

"*Her hand*," i.e., the left hand, as is shown by the
antithesis, "her right hand," which follows. On the
form תִּשְׁלַחְנָה, the third pers. fem. sing. with נה attached,
to distinguish it the more clearly from the second pers.,
see the remarks
on Exo_1:10. הַלְמוּת עֲמֵלִים, *hammer* or *mallet of the hard
workers*, is a large heavy hammer. For the purpose of
depicting the boldness and greatness of the deed, the
words are crowded together in the second
hemistich: הלם, to hammer, or smite with the
hammer; מחק, ἅπ. λεγ., to smite in pieces, smite
through; מחץ, to smite or dash in pieces; חלף, to pierce or
bore through. The heaping up of the words
in Jdg_5:27answers the same purpose. They do not
"express the delight of a satisfied thirst for revenge," but
simply bring out the thought that Sisera, who was for
years the terror of Israel, was now struck dead with a
single blow. בַּאֲשֶׁר כָּרַע, at the place where he bowed,

---

[37] From "Women in the Bible Books"

there he fell שָׁדוּד, overpowered and destroyed. In
conclusion, the singer refers once more in the last
strophe (Jdg 5:28-30) to the mother of Sisera, as she
waited impatiently for the return of her son, and
foreboded his death, whilst the prudent princesses who
surrounded her sought to cheer her with the prospect of a
rich arrival of booty. From "Women in the Bible
Books"[38]

Jdg 5:27 At her feet he bowed, he fell, he lay. At her feet
he bowed, he fell. Where he bowed, there he fell down
dead.
Jdg 5:28 Through the window she looked out, and cried:
Sisera's mother looked through the lattice. Why is his
chariot so long in coming? Why do the wheels of his
chariots wait?
Jdg 5:29 Her wise ladies answered her, Yes, she returned
answer to herself,
Jdg 5:30 Have they not found, have they not divided the
spoil? A lady, two ladies to every man; to Sisera a spoil
of dyed garments, A spoil of dyed garments
embroidered, Of dyed garments embroidered on both
sides, on the necks of the spoil?
Jdg 5:31 So let all your enemies perish, LORD, but let
those who love him be as the sun when it rises forth in
its strength. The land had rest forty years. (KJV)

5:24–27 Most blessed of women. **Jael** is a heroine for
killing Sisera (see 4:17–22). **Between her feet he sank,
he fell**. Chapter 4 tells us that Sisera already was lying

---

[38] From "Women in the Bible Books"

down, asleep, when Jael struck him (4:21). The poem is probably speaking metaphorically, repeating graphic, emotive language to make its point, namely, that a woman triumphed over this great warrior.

5:28–30 The mother of Sisera is a pitiable figure, but these verses highlight Jael's achievement: rather than bringing great plunder to impress his women, Sisera lay dead at another woman's feet. **A womb or two**. A crude reference to captured women.[39]

Was Jael A heartless woman? Robinson "Opening Up[40]

So what should we make of Jael; was she a heartless murdering woman who became God's tool for justice? There is no doubting the fact that she was not a woman to be scorned! But faced with the choice of giving refuge to a man who murdered, raped and pillaged God's people or bringing his life to a swift end she chose an option that, in the long run, would be less violent. It is true that she lulled Sisera into a false sense of security, which does lay her open to the charge of being treacherous. But when faced with a choice, Jael sided with God's people and in doing so she was used by God to bring about their deliverance.

These events are set in dark and violent times which called for desperate measures. Sisera was a ruthless man who

---

[39] Crossway Bibles. (2008). *The ESV Study Bible* (447–448). Wheaton, IL: Crossway Bibles.
[40] Robinson, S. J. (2006). *Opening up Judges*. Opening Up Commentary (29–30). Leominster: Day One Publications.

lived by the sword and perished by the sword (see Matt. 26:52). And Jael implemented some rough justice when it was in short supply. She brought a reign of terror to an end and that is why Deborah rejoiced at her actions and called her 'most blessed of women' (5:24).

Daughters of Israel – Women's Impact as Eishet Chayel

Webster's Definition:

Handmaiden- A woman or girl servant or attendant – that which accompanies in a useful but subordinate capacity.

Servant – A person ardently devoted to another or to a cause, creed etc.

YHWH is raising up handmaidens in these last days to be vessels for His glory.

(Luk 1:48 TLV) For He has looked with care upon the humble state **of His maidservant**. For behold, from now on all generations will call me blessed.

Servant/HandmaidenG1401

δοῦλος

doúlos; gen. doúlou, masc. noun. A slave, one who is in a permanent relation of servitude to another, his will being altogether consumed in the will of the other (Mat_8:9; Mat_20:27; Mat_24:45-46). Generally one serving, bound to serve, in bondage (Rom_6:16-17).

Handmaiden/Maidservant – Also translated in the Greek, Bondman, Servant or Bondservant

(II) Metaphorically spoken of voluntary service, a
servant, implying obedience, devotion (Joh_15:15;
Rom_6:16). Implying modesty (2Co_4:5); in praise of
modesty (Mat_20:27; Mar_10:44). Spoken of the true
followers and worshipers of God, e.g., a servant of God,
either of agents sent from God, as Moses (Rev_15:3; see
Jos_1:1) or prophets (Rev_10:7; Rev_11:18; Sept.:
Jos_24:29; Jer_7:25), or simply of the worshipers of God
(Rev_2:20; Rev_7:3; Rev_19:5; Sept.: Psa_34:22;
Psa_134:1); the followers and ministers of Christ
(Eph_6:6; 2Ti_2:24); especially applied to the Apostles
(Rom_1:1; Gal_1:10; 2Pe_1:1; Jud_1:1). Used instead of
the personal pron. in the oriental style of addressing a
superior (Luk_2:29; Act_4:29; Sept.: 1Sa_3:9-10;
Psa_19:12). In respect of things, one such as the servant
of sin who indulges in or is addicted to something
(Joh_8:34; Rom_6:16-17; 2Pe_2:19).

**Lk 1:26-38 Miriam/Mary yielded herself totally to
YHWH wills for her life as His handmaiden:**

(Luk 1:26 TLV) Then in the sixth month, the angel
Gabriel was sent by Adonai into a town in the Galilee
named Natzeret

(Luk 1:27 TLV) and to a virgin engaged to a man
named Joseph, of the house of David. The virgin's name
was Miriam.

(Luk 1:28 TLV) And coming to her, the angel said,
"Shalom, favored one! Adonai is with you."

(Luk 1:29 TLV) But at the message, she was perplexed

and kept wondering what kind of greeting this might be.

(Luk 1:30 TLV) The angel spoke to her, "Do not be afraid, Miriam, for you have found favor with God.

(Luk 1:31 TLV) Behold, you will become pregnant and give birth to a son, and you shall call His name Yeshua.

(Luk 1:32 TLV) He will be great and will be called Ben-Elyon. Adonai Elohim will give Him the throne of David, His father.

(Luk 1:33 TLV) He shall reign over the house of Jacob for all eternity, and His kingdom will be without end."

(Luk 1:34 TLV) Miriam said to the angel, "How can this be, since I am not intimate with a man?"

(Luk 1:35 TLV) And responding, the angel said to her, "The Ruach ha-Kodesh will come upon you, and the power of Elyon will overshadow you. Therefore, the Holy One being born will be called Ben-Elohim.

(Luk 1:36 TLV) Behold, even your relative Elizabeth has conceived a son in her old age; and the one who was called barren is six months pregnant.

(Luk 1:37 TLV) For nothing will be impossible with God."

(Luk 1:38 TLV) So Miriam said, "Behold, the servant of Adonai. Let it be done to me according to your word." And the angel left her.

Jeremiah 18:2-4 – His vessel. How can we be YHWH's handmaiden to glorify Him? When a vessel was marred, it was not thrown away, the clay was crushed together and returned to the wheel and the work began again. This continued until the clay took

**on the shape the potter attended. Be clay in the
Potters hand, let him mold you and make you the
Women of YHWH you were meant to be.**

(Jer 18:1 TLV) The word came to Jeremiah from
Adonai, saying:

(Jer 18:2 TLV) "Arise, and go down to the potter's
house, and there I will cause you to hear My words."

(Jer 18:3 TLV) So I went down to the potter's house,
and there he was making a work on the wheels.

(Jer 18:4 TLV) Whenever the pot that he was making
from the clay became flawed in the hand of the potter, he
remade it into another pot, as it pleased the potter to
make.

**YHWH is not looking for ability, but for availability
and then He will give the ability and all glory will go
to Him.**

I. Characteristics of YHWH's Handmaiden

Proverbs 31:10-31

1. Morally perfect – vs 10
2. valuable- vs 10
3. Trustworthy –vs 11
4. Inherently good and true – vs 12
5. Ingenious, proficient – vs 13
6. Thrifty – vs 14
7. Dutiful-considerate-vs 15
8. Versatile-judicious – vs 16

9. Tireless- healthy-vs 17
10. Joyful-efficient-vs 18
11. Watchful-cautious – vs. 18
12. Skillful & Thrifty-vs 19
13. Charitable & benevolent-vs20
14. Generous & Merciful-vs 20
15. Fearless, proficient – vs 21
16. Clever at decorating and furnishing
17. Refined in taste-vs 22
18. Respected & popular – vs 23
19. Industrious & prosperous-vs 24
20. Dependable-honest –vs25
21. Confident-hopeful-vs 25
22. Wise-discreet – vs 26
23. Kind and understanding-vs 26
24. Prudent- Practical-vs 27
25. Energetic-ever active-vs 27
26. An ideal wife & mother –vs 28
27. Honored by her family-vs 27-28
28. Excels in Virtue-vs 28
29. God fearing- humble – vs 30
30. Deserving-successful – vs 31
31. Honored by the public- vs 31

Amplified Bible footnote on the above scripture:

It is most unfortunate that this description of Gods ideal
woman is usually confined in readers minds merely to it
literal sense. Her ability as a homemaker, as in the
picture of Martha of Bethan in Lk 10:38-42. But it is
obvious that far more than that is meant. When the
summary of what makes her value far above rubies is

given (Prov 31:30) **it is her spiritual life only that is mentioned.** One can almost hear the voice of Yeshua/Yeshua saying "Mary has chosen the good portion. which shall not be taken away from her" **"Many daughters have done...nobly and well//but you excel them all" What a glowing description here recorded of this woman in private life this capable intelligent and virtuous woman of Proverbs 31.**

It means she had done more than Miriam, the one who led a nation of women in praise to YHWH (Ex 15:20-21), Deborah, the patriotic military advisor (Judges 4:4-10) Ruth the women of constancy (Ruth 1:16). Hannah, the ideal mother (! Sam 1:20), the Shunamite, the hospitable women (11 Kings 4:8-10) Huldah, the women who revealed YHWH's secret message to nation leaders (11 Kings 22:14) and even more than Queen Esther, the women who risked sacrificing her life for her people (Esther 4:16). In what way did she excel them all? In her spiritual and practical devotion to YHWH, which permeated every area and relationship of her life. All seven of the Christian/Messianic virtues (11 Peter 1:5) are there, like a colored thread in a tapestry. Her secret which is open to everyone is the Ruach HaKodesh climax to the story and to this book. In Proverbs 31:30 it becomes clear that the "reverent and worshipful fear of the Lord" which is the beginning (the chief and choice part of Wisdom (Prov 9:10) is put forth as the true foundation for a life which is valued by YHWH and her husband as "far above rubies or pearls" Proverbs 31:10

II. Crowning Qualities of YHWH's Handmaiden

1 Samuel 1:10-15 – Hannah, a woman of prayer, poured out her heart to YHWH. A woman of faith who kept her word.

(1Sa 1:10 TLV) While her soul was bitter, she prayed to Adonai and wept.

(1Sa 1:11 TLV) So she made a vow and said, "Adonai-Tzva'ot, if You will indeed look upon the affliction of Your handmaid, remember me and not forget Your handmaid, but grant Your handmaid a son, then I will give him to Adonai all the days of his life and no razor will ever touch his head."

(1Sa 1:12 TLV) It came to pass, as she prayed long before Adonai, that Eli was watching her mouth.

(1Sa 1:13 TLV) Now Hannah was praying in her heart—only her lips were moving, but her voice could not be heard. So Eli thought she was drunk.

(1Sa 1:14 TLV) Then Eli said to her, "How long will you be drunk? Get rid of your wine!"

(1Sa 1:15 TLV) But in response Hannah said, "No, my lord, I am a woman with an oppressed spirit! I haven't been drinking wine or beer. Instead I've been pouring out my soul before Adonai.

(1Sa 1:16 TLV) Don't consider your handmaid a wicked woman. For out of my great anguish and grief I've been praying until now."

(1Sa 1:17 TLV) Then Eli responded, "Go in shalom, and may the God of Israel grant your petition that you asked of Him."

(1Sa 1:18 TLV) "May your maidservant find favor in your eyes," she said. So the woman went her way; she ate, and her countenance was no longer dejected.

(1Sa 1:19 TLV) They rose up early in the morning and worshipped before Adonai, then went back to their home to Ramah. Then Elkanah was intimate with his wife Hannah, and Adonai remembered her.

(1Sa 1:20 TLV) So it came to pass at the turn of the year that Hannah conceived and gave birth to a son. She called his name Samuel, "because I have asked Adonai for him."

Esther 4:10-17 – A woman of courage. YHWH give you the strength to do what He has called you to do.

(Est 4:11 TLV) "All the king's servants and the people of the king's provinces fully understand that for anyone, man or woman, who approaches the king in the inner courtyard without being summoned, he has one law— that he be put to death, unless the king extends his golden scepter permitting him to live. But I have not been summoned to come to the king for 30 days."

(Est 4:12 TLV) So they conveyed Esther's words to Mordecai.

(Est 4:13 TLV) Mordecai told them to reply to Esther with this answer, "Do not think in your soul that you will escape in the king's household more than all the Jews.

(Est 4:14 TLV) For if you remain silent at this time, relief and deliverance will arise for the Jews from

another place—but you and your father's house will
perish. Who knows whether you have attained royal
status for such a time as this?"

(Est 4:15 TLV) Esther sent this to reply to Mordecai,

(Est 4:16 TLV) "Go! Gather together all the Jews who
are in Shushan and fast for me. Do not eat or drink for
three days, night or day. My maids and I will fast in the
same way. Afterwards, I will go in to the king, even
though it is not according to the law. So if I perish, I
perish!"

(Est 4:17 TLV) So Mordecai left and did all that Esther
commanded him.

**Lk 2:36-37- Anna, a Prophetess and Intercessor –
Hebrew – hannebiah –a woman who prophesies**

(Luk 2:36 TLV) Now Anna, a daughter of Phanuel of
the tribe of Asher, was a prophetess. She was well
advanced in age, having lived with a husband only seven
years

(Luk 2:37 TLV) and then as a widow until age eighty-
four. She never left the Temple, serving night and day
with fasting and prayers.

(Luk 2:38 TLV) And coming up at that very instant, she
began praising God and speaking about the Child to all
those waiting for the redemption of Jerusalem.

Lk 10: 39-42- Miriam and Martha – Hunger for the Living Torah

(Luk 10:38 TLV) Now while they were traveling, Yeshua entered a certain village; and a woman named Martha welcomed Him into her house.

(Luk 10:39 TLV) She had a sister called Miriam, who was seated at the Master's feet, listening to His teaching.

(Luk 10:40 TLV) But Martha was distracted with much serving; so she approached Yeshua and said, "Master, doesn't it concern you that my sister has left me to serve alone? Then tell her to help me!"

(Luk 10:41 TLV) But answering her, the Lord said, "Martha, Martha, you are anxious and bothered about many things;

(Luk 10:42 TLV) but only one thing is necessary. For Miriam has chosen the good part, which will not be taken away from her."

Acts 16:14 – Lydia, industrious and creative

(Act 16:14 TLV) A woman named Lydia—a seller of purple cloth from the city of Thyatira, a God-fearer— was listening. The Lord opened her heart to respond to what Paul was saying.

III. Modesty – Greek- Kosmious – orderly, well arranged, decent, modest, a harmonious arrangement

Genesis 24:65 – Rebekkah - Modest, not a flirt

(Gen 24:65 TLV) Then she said to the servant, "Who is that man there who is walking in the field—to meet us?" The servant said, "He is my master." So she took the veil and covered herself.

1 Timothy 2:9-10 – Greek, ardos, sense of shame, or honor and regard for others, respect, reverence, self-restraint, modesty or bashfulness. Her witness to unsaved (especially husband)

(1Ti 2:9 TLV) Likewise, women are to adorn themselves in appropriate clothing with modesty and sound judgment—not in seductive hairstyles and gold or pearls or costly clothing,
(1Ti 2:10 TLV) but what is suitable for women claiming godliness, through good deeds.

1.	**Submits to and obeys husband who walks in the Word.**
2.	**Obeys the Torah/Word**
3.	**Has chaste conversation**
4.	**Let's not the outward adorning be the chief aim in life.**
5.	**Let's the inner man be adorned more than the outward man.**
6.	**Trusts YHWH**
7.	**Does well**
8.	**Lives faithful to the husband as there is no fear of being found guilty of infidelity.**

Galatians 5:22-23 – She's a woman who walks love and manifests the fruit of the spirit in her life.

(Gal 5:22 TLV) But the fruit of the Ruach is love, joy, peace, patience, kindness, goodness, faithfulness,

(Gal 5:23 TLV) gentleness, and self-control—against such things there is no law.

(1Co 13:4 TLV) Love is patient, love is kind, it does not envy, it does not brag, it is not puffed up,

(1Co 13:5 TLV) it does not behave inappropriately, it does not seek its own way, it is not provoked, it keeps no account of wrong,

(1Co 13:6 TLV) it does not rejoice over injustice but rejoices in the truth;

(1Co 13:7 TLV) it bears all things, it believes all things, it hopes all things, it endures all things.

(1Co 13:8 TLV) Love never fails—but where there are prophecies, they will pass away; where there are tongues, they will cease; where there is knowledge, it will pass away.

(1Co 13:13 TLV) But now these three remain—faith, hope, and love. And the greatest of these is love

One of the "'Sins" that women need to deal with and guard against is the sin of PRIDE!
Here is an excellent list that I have used in my prayer time to pinpoint areas in my life where pride has

reared its ugly head. This list was put together by Nancy Leigh DeMoss of <u>www.lifeaction.org</u>.[41]

How can we know if our hearts are proud or broken?

Proud people focus on the failures of others; they have a critical, fault-finding spirit. They look at everyone else's faults with a microscope, but their own with a telescope. By contrast, *broken people* are overwhelmed with a sense of their own spiritual need. Therefore, they can esteem all others better than themselves.

Proud people have to prove that they are right; but *broken people* are willing to yield the right to be right.

Proud people are protective of their time, their rights, and their reputation. But *broken people* have yielded their rights.

Proud people want to be served and to be a success. But *broken people* desire to serve others and to make them a success.[42]

Proud people have a drive to be recognized and appreciated. They get wounded when others are

---

[41] This list was put together by Nancy Leigh DeMoss of www.lifeaction.org.

[42] This list was put together by Nancy Leigh DeMoss of www.lifeaction.org.

promoted and they are overlooked. But *broken
people* have a sense of their own unworthiness and are
thrilled that God would use them at all; they rejoice
when others are lifted up.

Proud people are quick to blame others for their
problems. And they are unapproachable or defensive
when criticized. But *broken people* are quick to see
where they were wrong in a situation; they receive
criticism with a humble, teachable spirit.

Proud people are quick to take offense; but *broken
people* are quick to forgive and overlook offenses.

Proud people wait for others to come and ask
forgiveness when there is a misunderstanding or conflict
in a relationship. *Broken people* take the initiative to be
reconciled when there is a conflict; they race to the cross
and see who can get there first, no matter how wrong the
other may have been.

Proud people compare themselves to others and think
they are doing all right. They don't think they have
anything to repent of. But *broken people* compare
themselves to the holiness of God; they feel a desperate
need for His mercy and realize they have need of a
continual heart attitude of repentance.

Proud people don't think they need revival--but they're
sure that everyone else does! *Broken people* continually
sense their need for a fresh encounter with God.

Why would anyone want to be broken, any more than someone would want to sign up for surgery or suffering? God's Word teaches that brokenness brings blessedness. Yeshua said, "Blessed are the poor in spirit" --i.e., the "broken ones," those who recognize that they are spiritually bankrupt and poverty-stricken.

IV. Liberality or Giver-Using your Gifts.

Exodus 35:25 – Women used talents to weave fine linen for the Mishkan/Tabernacle

(Exo 35:25 TLV) Also all the women who were wise-hearted spun with their hands, and brought what they had woven—the blue, purple, scarlet and fine linen.

(Exo 35:26 TLV) All the women whose heart stirred them up with wisdom spun the goat hair.

Proverbs 31:20 – Compassion for the poor

Pro 31:20 She opens her arms to the poor; yes, she extends her hands to the needy.

Lk 8:2-3- They will give all they have of themselves to The Master Yeshua

(Luk 8:3 TLV) Joanna, the wife of Kuza, Herod's finance minister; Susanna; and many others—were supporting them out of their own resources.

John 12:3 – Nothing too costly to give to minister to Him

(Joh 12:3 TLV) Then Miriam took a pound of very expensive oil of pure nard and anointed Yeshua's feet, and she wiped His feet dry with her hair. Now the house was filled with the fragrance of the oil.

Acts 9:39 – Example of Dorcas – Dorcas was loved because of the help she gave to the widows. She was industrious, a leader well loved.

(Act 9:39 TLV) So Peter got up and went with them. When he arrived, they took him to the upstairs room. All the widows were crying, showing all the tunics and other clothing Dorcas had made while she was with them.

V. Wisdom and Virtue

Proverbs 11:16 – Hebrew- Chin – a woman full of favor and grace

(Pro 11:16 TLV) A gracious woman gains honor, but ruthless men seize riches.

H2580

חֵן

chên

khane From H2603; *graciousness*, that is, subjectively
(*kindness, favor*) or objectively (*beauty*): - favour, grace
(-ious), pleasant, precious, [well-] favoured.

**Proverbs 12:4 – Hebrew –Chayel – strength of mind
or body, a morally strong women is a crown to her
husband, but the weakling contracts and
communicates such disease as being rottenness to the
bone.**

 (Pro 12:4 TLV) A virtuous wife is her husband's
crown, but a dishonoring one is like rottenness in his
bones.

H2428-Virtuous

חַיִל

Chayil *khah'-yil*

From H2342; probably a *force*, whether of men, means
or other resources;
an *army, wealth, virtue, valor, strength:* - able, activity,
(+) army, band of men (soldiers), company, (great)
forces, goods, host, might, power, riches, strength,
strong, substance, train, (+) valiant (-ly), valour, virtuous
(-ly), war, worthy (-ily).

H5850 –Crown – An emblem of honor

עֲטָרָה

ʿăṭârâh

at-aw-raw'
From H5849; a *crown:* - crown.

H7538-=Rotteness
רקב
râqâb
raw-kawb'
From H7537; *decay* (by *caries*): - rottenness (thing).

Proverbs 14:1 – The wise women through proper management increases the property, furniture, food and raiment of the household, but the thriftless women causes the blessings to depart

Pro 14:1 Every wise women builds her house, but the foolish one tears it down with her own hands.

(Rth 3:11 TLV) Now my daughter, do not be afraid! Everything you propose, I will do for you, for everyone in town knows that you are a woman of valor.

VI – Handmaidens Ministry

11 Kings 4:10 -17– Hospitality to God's prophet. She gave her best and YHWH blessed!

(2Ki 4:10 TLV) Please, let's make a little walled room on the roof, and let's put there a bed, a table, a chair, and a lampstand for him. Then whenever he comes to us, he can stay there."
(2Ki 4:11 TLV) One day he came there, and retired to

the upper chamber and lay down there.

(2Ki 4:12 TLV) Then he said to Gehazi his servant, "Call this Shunammite woman." When he had called her, she stood before him.

(2Ki 4:13 TLV) He said to him, "Tell her: Behold, you have gone to all this trouble for us. What can be done for you? Can something be communicated to the king or to the commander of the army for you?" She answered, "I am living among my own people."

(2Ki 4:14 TLV) So he asked, "Then what should be done for her?" Then Gehazi answered, "In fact, she has no son, and her husband is old."

(2Ki 4:15 TLV) "Call her," he said. And when he had called her, she stood in the doorway.

(2Ki 4:16 TLV) Then he said, "At this season next year, you will be embracing a son." But she said, "No, my lord, do not lie to your handmaid, man of God."

(2Ki 4:17 TLV) Nevertheless, the woman conceived and bore a son during that season the following year, just as Elisha had told her.

Proverbs 31:20 – She respects and loves both YHWH and the poor, and is good to all in need

(Pro 31:20 TLV) She spreads out her palms to the poor, and extends her hands to the needy.

Matthew 27:55-56 – To their honor, these women showed more courage and affectionate concern for there Master then the men who had promised to die for Him. They ministered of their substance. (KJV)

(Mat 27:55 TLV) Many women were there, watching from a distance. They had followed Yeshua from the Galilee, serving Him.

(Mat 27:56 TLV) Among them were Miriam from Magdala, Miriam the mother of Jacob and Joseph, and the mother of Zebedee's sons.

(Mar 14:3 TLV) And while Yeshua was in Bethany at the house of Simon ha-Metzora, reclining at the table, a woman came with an alabaster jar of very expensive oil of pure nard. Breaking open the jar, she poured it over His head.

(Mar 14:4 TLV) But some got angry and said among themselves, "Why was this fragrant oil wasted?

(Mar 14:5 TLV) It could have been sold for over three hundred denarii, and the money given to the poor!" And they kept scolding her.

(Mar 14:6 TLV) But Yeshua said, "Leave her alone. Why do you cause trouble for her? She's done Me a mitzvah.

(Mar 14:7 TLV) For you always have the poor with you, and you can do good for them whenever you want; but you won't always have Me.

(Mar 14:8 TLV) She did what she could—she came beforehand to anoint My body for burial.

(Mar 14:9 TLV) Amen, I tell you, wherever the Good News is proclaimed in all the world, what she has done will also be told in memory of her."

Lk 7:37-38 – Women who ministered to the Masters needs

(Luk 7:37 TLV) And behold, a woman in the town who was a sinner, when she discovered that Yeshua was reclining at the Pharisee's home, brought an alabaster jar of perfume.

(Luk 7:38 TLV) As she stood behind Him at His feet, weeping, she began to drench His feet with tears and kept wiping them with her head of hair. Then she was kissing His feet and anointing them with perfume.

Romans 16:1-2- Example- Phoebe was a Deaconess, attended to female converts, helping them to get ready for the Mikvah/baptism, to visit the sick and those in prison who attended to all parts of the Congregation of Messiah among the women, which could not be performed by men, who probably was the bearer of the epistle to Rome.

In an age where feminism is an issue, it should be noted not only that this woman held a prominent office in the Cenchrean congregation, but that the word "*diakonos*" is a masculine, not a feminine, form. Phoebe was a "deacon," not a "deaconess" (as some English versions render the word). See 1Ti_3:8-13 for the qualifications of a *shammash*. – Complete New Testament Jewish

Bible Commentary David Stearns

(Rom 16:1 TLV) Now I recommend to you our sister
Phoebe—who is a servant-leader of Messiah's
community at Cenchrea—

(Rom 16:2 TLV) so you may receive her in the Lord, in
a way worthy of kedoshim, and help her in whatever
matter she may need from you. For she herself has
become a patroness of many, including me as well.

**Romans 16: -3-5 – Priscilla, along with her husband
had a Congregation in their home.**

(Rom 16:3 TLV) Greet Prisca and Aquila, my fellow
workers in Messiah Yeshua,

(Rom 16:4 TLV) who risked their own necks for my
life. Not only I give them thanks, but also all of
Messiah's communities among the Gentiles.

(Rom 16:5 TLV) Greet also the community that meets
in their house. Greet Epaenetus whom I dearly love, who
is the first fruit in Asia for Messiah.

Priscilla and Aquila. See Act_18:1-3. Continuing the
theme of Rom_16:1, the mention of the woman first may
indicate her greater prominence (see Act_18:18). It is not
known on what occasion they **risked their necks** for
Sha'ul; they may have had such a role in the Ephesus
disturbance of Act_19:23-40, since it seems to have been
there that they hosted a congregation in their home (see
1Co_16:19, Act_19:10), just as they did in Rome.

The congregation that meets in their house. The
Greek word for "congregation" is "*ekklêsia*," which most
English translations render "church" (see Mat_16:18).
"*Ekklêsia*" means "called-out ones" and thus refers to the
people, not a building, as is clear from this verse. It
sometimes means the entire number of believers united
with the Messiah throughout history, or all the believers
in a particular city (either at a particular time or over a
period of time), but here it means a local congregation.
The New Testament considers it the norm for believers
to meet together regularly (compare 1Co_16:1-2,
Heb_10:24-25). Complete New Testament Jewish Bible
Commentary David Stearns

**Romans 16:6 – Miriam ministered to the Apostles
needs. Vs 13 Rufus mother was like a mother to Shaul**

(Rom 16:6 TLV) Greet Miriam, who has worked hard
for you.

(Rom 16:13 TLV) Greet Rufus, chosen in the Lord, and
his mother—who was also a mother to me.

**How can we minister to Yeshua as YHWH's
handmaidens?**

Mat 25:32 Before him all the nations will be gathered,
and he will separate them one from another, as a (Mat
25:34 TLV) Then the King will say to those on His
right, 'Come, you who are blessed by My Father, inherit
the kingdom prepared for you from the foundation of the

world.

(Mat 25:35 TLV) For I was hungry and you gave Me
something to eat; I was thirsty and you gave Me
something to drink; I was a stranger and you invited Me
in;

(Mat 25:36 TLV) I was naked and you clothed Me; I
was sick and you visited Me; I was in prison and you
came to Me.'

(Mat 25:37 TLV) "Then the righteous will answer Him,
'Lord, when did we see You hungry and feed You? Or
thirsty and give You something to drink?

(Mat 25:38 TLV) And when did we see You a stranger
and invite You in? Or naked and clothe You?

(Mat 25:39 TLV) When did we see You sick, or in
prison, and come to You?'

(Mat 25:40 TLV) "And answering, the King will say to
them, 'Amen, I tell you, whatever you did to one of the
least of these My brethren, you did it to Me.'

Galatians 6:1-2 – Sympathy, show mercy and love and do not browbeat a fallen brother/sister

Gal 6:1 Brothers, even if a man is caught in some fault,
you who are spiritual must restore such a one in a spirit
of gentleness; looking to yourself so that you also aren't
tempted.

Gal 6:2 Bear one another's burdens, and so fulfill the
Torah of Messiah. (HNV)

Galatians 6:9-10 – be good to all mankind – friends and enemies

(Gal 6:1 TLV) Brothers and sisters, if someone is caught doing something wrong, you who are directed by the Ruach, restore such a person in a spirit of gentleness—looking closely at yourself so you are not tempted also.

(Gal 6:2 TLV) Bear one another's burdens, and in this way you fulfill the Torah of Messiah.

Matthew 10:38-42 – Attitude toward new believers and children, the minutest details of goodness will not go unrewarded.

(Mat 10:38 TLV) And whoever does not take up his cross and follow after Me isn't worthy of Me.

(Mat 10:39 TLV) He who finds his life will lose it, and he who loses his life for My sake will find it.

(Mat 10:40 TLV) "He who receives you receives Me, and he who receives Me receives the One who sent Me.

(Mat 10:41 TLV) He who receives a prophet in the name of a prophet shall receive a prophet's reward, and he who receives a tzaddik in the name of a tzaddik shall receive a tzaddik's reward.

(Mat 10:42 TLV) And whoever gives to one of these little ones even a cup of cold water in the name of a disciple, amen I tell you, he shall never lose his reward."

Ephesians 6:7-8 – Serve as unto YHWH who sees all

(Eph 6:7 TLV) Serve with a positive attitude, as to the
Lord and not to men—

(Eph 6:8 TLV) knowing that whatever good each one
does, this he will receive back from the Lord, whether
slave or free.

Hebrews 12:28-29 – Serve YHWH with fear (reverence, Godly fear)

(Heb 10:28 TLV) Anyone who rejected the Torah of
Moses dies without compassion on the word of two or
three witnesses.

(Heb 10:29 TLV) How much more severe do you think
the punishment will be for the one who has trampled
Ben-Elohim underfoot, and has regarded as unholy the
blood of the covenant by which he was made holy, and
has insulted the Spirit of grace?

John 12:26 – The Father honors those who serve Yeshua

(Joh 12:26 TLV) If any man serves Me, he must follow
Me; and where I am, there also will My servant be. If
anyone serves Me, the Father will honor him.

Colossians 3:23-25 – Your reward is from YHWH

(Col 3:23 TLV) Whatever you do, work at it from the soul, as for the Lord and not for people.

(Col 3:24 TLV) For you know that from the Lord you will receive the inheritance as a reward. It is to the Lord Messiah you are giving service.

(Col 3:25 TLV) For the one doing wrong will be paid back for what he did wrong, and there is no favoritism.

THERE IS JOY IN BEING YHWH'S HANDMAIDEN!

Psalm 40:8 (9) – We should delight in serving YHWH

(Psa 40:9 TLV) I delight to do Your will, O my God. Yes, Your Torah is within my being."

Psalm 126:5-6 – Law of sowing and reaping service, even though sometimes you will be hurt by people if you keep your eyes on Yeshua you will reap with JOY!

(Psa 126:5 TLV) Those who sow in tears will reap with a song of joy.

(Psa 126:6 TLV) Whoever keeps going out weeping, carrying his bag of seed, will surely come back with a song of joy, carrying his sheaves.

Who is this Eishet Chayel?

- She is the single mom struggling to make ends meet.
- She is the wife who stands by her husband in good times and bad.
- She is the mother who never gives up on her wayward children, even when her heart is breaking inside.
- She is the widow who just lost her soul mate.
- She is the mother with a child who has a terminal illness, but whose hope and faith never waiver.
- She is a soldier fighting in a foreign land.
- She is often considered weak, but she has the inner strength of a warrior.
- She is the prayer warrior that no one sees praying for the Body of Messiah
- She is a woman, wife, mother, grandmother.
- She is the one who was rejected, but never gave up.
- She is thin, fat, short, tall, blonde, brunette a tireless worker for the Kingdom of God
- She has more scars inside of her from past hurts and abuse that only God can see.
- She is a servant, a healer, a doctor, a counselor, a homemaker, an office worker, a nurse or a doctor, a soldier a missionary.
- She is often misunderstood and unappreciated.
- Yet she is God's mighty handmaiden and to be reckoned with in these last days as one who serves her God with all her spirit, soul and body, even though she gets little or no recognition from those she serves, she does it with gladness because she

knows her reward is great......She is God's virtuous women.

Biblical Women from the Tenach-Intertestamental Period to Second Temple Apostolic Renewed Covenant Period.[43]

The generic term "man" includes women. In the narrative of the creation (Gen_1:26, Gen_1:27) Adam is a collective term for mankind. It may signify human being, male or female, or humanity entire. "God said, let us make man ... and let them" (Gen_1:26), the latter word "them" defining "man" in the former clause. So, in Gen_1:27, "in the image of God created he him; male and female created he them," "them" being synonymous with "him."

In the Creative Plan

Whatever interpretation the latest scholarship may give to the story of women's formation from the rib of man (Gen_2:21-24), the passage indicates, most profoundly, the inseparable unity and fellowship of her life with his. Far more than being a mere assistant, "helper" (עזר, *'ēzer* "help" "helper" Gen_2:18), she is man's complement, essential to the perfection of his being. Without her he is not *man* in the generic fullness of that term. Priority of creation may indicate headship, but not, as theologians have so uniformly affirmed, superiority.

---

[43] Outline from ISBE=International Standard Bible Encyclopedia woman
http://www.internationalstandardbible.com/W/women.html

Dependence indicates difference of function, not
inferiority. Human values are estimated in terms of the
mental and spiritual. Man and women are endowed for
equality, and are mutually interdependent. Physical
strength and prowess cannot be rated in the same
category with moral courage and the capacity to endure
ill-treatment, sorrow and pain; and in these latter
qualities women has always proved herself the superior.
Man's historic treatment of women, due to his conceit,
ignorance or moral perversion, has taken her inferiority
for granted, and has thus necessitated it by her
enslavement and degradation. The narrative of the Fall
(Gen 3) ascribes to women supremacy of influence, for
through her stronger personality man was led to
disobedience of God's command. Her penalty for such
ill-fated leadership was that her husband should "rule
over" her (Gen 3:16), not because of any inherent
superiority on his part, but because of her loss of prestige
and power through sin. In that act she forfeited the
respect and confidence which entitled her to equality of
influence in family affairs. Her recovery from the curse
of subjection was to come through the afflictive suffering
of maternity, for, as Paul puts it, "she shall be saved
(from the penalty of her transgression) through her childbearing" (1Ti 2:15).

Sin, both in man and women, has been universally the
cause of women's degradation. All history must be
interpreted in the light of man's consequent mistaken
estimate of her endowments, worth and rightful
place. The ancient Hebrews never entirely lost the light
of their original revelation, and, more than any other

oriental race, held women in high esteem, honor and affection. Yeshua's teachings and spirit prevail, she is made the loved companion, confidante and adviser of her husband.

In The Ancient Near East[44]

1. Prominence of Women:
Under the Hebrew system, the position of women was in marked contrast with her status in surrounding heathen nations. Her liberties were greater, her employments more varied and important, her social standing more respectful and commanding. The divine law given on Sinai (Exo_20:12) required children to honor the mother equally with the father. "the law of thy mother" (Pro_1:8; Pro_6:20) was not to be forsaken, while contempt for the same merited the curse of God (Pro_19:26; Pro_20:20; Pro_30:11, Pro_30:17).

2. Social Equality:
Additional evidence of women's social equality comes from the fact that men and women feasted together without restriction. Women shared in the sacred meals and great annual feasts (Deu_16:11, Deu_16:14); in wedding festivities (Joh_2:1-3); in the fellowship of the family meal (Joh_12:3). They could appear, as Sarah did in the court of Egypt, unveiled (Gen_12:11, Gen_12:14). Rebekah (Gen_24:16; compare Gen_24:65), Rachel

---

[44] Outline from ISBE=International Standard Bible Encyclopedia woman http://www.internationalstandardbible.com/W/women.html

(Gen_29:11), Hannah (1Sa_1:13) appeared in public and
before suitors with uncovered faces

More honor was shown the courtesan than the
wife. Chastity and modesty, the choice inheritance of
Hebrew womanhood, were foreign to the Greek
conception of morality, and disappeared from Rome
when Greek culture and frivolity entered. The Greeks
made the shameless Phryne the model of the goddess
Aphrodite, and lifted their hands to public prostitutes
when they prayed in their temples. Under pagan culture
and heathen darkness women were universally subject to
inferior and degrading conditions. Every decline in her
status in the Hebrew commonwealth was due to the
incursion of foreign influence. The lapses of Hebrew
morality, especially in the court of Solomon and of
subsequent kings, occurred through the borrowing of
idolatrous and heathen customs from surrounding
nations (1Ki_11:1-8)

3. Marriage Laws:[45]

The Bible gives no sanction to dual or plural marriages.
The narrative in Gen_2:18-24 indicates that monogamy
was the divine ideal for man. The moral decline of the
generations antedating the Flood seems to have been
due, chiefly; to the growing disregard of the sanctity of
marriage. Lamech's taking of two wives (Gen_4:19) is

---

[45] Outline from ISBE=International Standard Bible Encyclopedia woman
http://www.internationalstandardbible.com/W/women.html

the first recorded infraction of the divine ideal. By
Noah's time polygamy had degenerated into promiscuous
inter-racial marriages of the most incestuous and illicit
kind (Gen_6:1-4; see SONS OF GOD). The subsequent
record ascribes marital infidelity and corruption to sin,
and affirms that the destruction of the race by the Flood
and the overthrow of Sodom and Gomorrah were God's
specific judgment on man's immorality. The dual
marriages of the Patriarchs were due, chiefly, to the
desire for children, and are not to be traced to divine
consent or approval. The laws of Moses regarding
chastity protected the sanctity of marriage (see
MARRIAGE), and indicated a higher regard for women
than prevailed in Gentile or other Semitic races
(Lev_18:6-20). They sought to safeguard her from the
sensual abominations prevalent among the Egyptians and
Canaanites (Lev 18). Kings were forbidden to "multiply
wives" (Deu_17:17). Concubinage in Israel was an
importation from heathenism.

Divorce was originally intended to protect the sanctity of
wedlock by outlawing the offender and his moral
offense. Its free extension to include any marital
infelicity met the stern rebuke of Jesus/Yeshua, who
declared that at the best it was a concession to human
infirmity and hardness of heart, and should be granted
only in case of adultery (Mat_5:32).

Hebrew women were granted a freedom in choosing a
husband not known elsewhere in the East (Gen_24:58).
Jewish tradition declares that a girl over 12 1/2 years of
age had the right to give herself in marriage. Vows made

by a daughter, while under age, could be annulled by the father (Num_30:3-5) or by the husband (Num_30:6-16). Whenever civil law made a concession to the customs of surrounding nations, as in granting the father power to sell a daughter into bondage, it sought to surround her with all possible protection (Deu_22:16 ff).

4. Inheritance:
The Mosaic Law prescribed that the father's estate, in case there were no sons, should pass to the daughters (Num_27:1-8). They were not permitted, however, to alienate the family inheritance by marrying outside their own tribe (Num_36:6-9). Such alien marriages were permissible only when the husband took the wife's family name (Neh_7:63). Unmarried daughters, not provided for in the father's will, were to be cared for by the eldest son (Gen_31:14, Gen_31:15). The bride's dowry, at marriage, was intended as a substitute for her share in the family estate. In rabbinical law, a century or more before Christ, it took the form of a settlement upon the wife and was considered obligatory. Provision for women under the ancient Mosaic Law was not inferior to her status under English law regarding landed estates.

5. Domestic Duties:[46]
Among the Hebrews, women administered the affairs of the home with a liberty and leadership unknown to other oriental peoples. Her domestic duties were more

---

[46] Outline from ISBE=International Standard Bible Encyclopedia woman
http://www.internationalstandardbible.com/W/women.html

independent, varied and honorable. She was not the slave
or menial of her husband. Her outdoor occupations were
congenial, healthful, extensive. She often tended the
flocks (Gen_29:6; Exo_2:16); spun the wool, and made
the clothing of the family
(Exo_35:26; Pro_31:19; 1Sa_2:19); contributed by her
weaving and needlework to its income and support
(Pro_31:14, Pro_31:24), and to charity (Act_9:39).
Women ground the grain (Mat_24:41); prepared the
meals (Gen_18:6; 2Sa_13:8; Joh_12:2); invited and
received guests (Jdg_4:18; 1Sa_25:18 ff; 2Ki_4:8-10);
drew water for household use (1Sa_9:11; Joh_4:7), for
guests and even for their camels (Gen_24:15-20).
Hebrew women enjoyed a freedom that corresponds
favorably with the larger liberties granted them in the
Christian era.

6. Dress and Ornaments:

That women were fond of decorations and display in
ancient as in modern times is clear from the reproof
administered by the prophet for their haughtiness and
excessive ornamentation (Isa_3:16). He bids them
"remove (the) veil, strip off the train," that they may be
better able to "grind meal" and attend to the other
womanly duties of the home (Isa_47:2). These prophetic
reproofs do not necessarily indicate general conditions,
but exceptional tendencies to extravagance and excess.
The ordinary dress of women was modest and simple,
consisting of loose flowing robes, similar to those worn
by men, and still in vogue among Orientals, chiefly the
mantle, shawl and veil (Rth_3:15; Isa_3:22, Isa_3:23).
The veil, however, was not worn for seclusion, as among

the Moslems. The extensive wardrobe and jewelry of
Hebrew women is suggested by the catalogue given
in Isa_3:18-24 : anklets, cauls, crescents, pendants,
bracelets, mufflers, head tires, ankle chains, sashes,
perfume-boxes, amulets, rings, nose-jewels, festival
robes, mantles, shawls, satchels, hand-mirrors, fine linen,
turbans, veils. The elaborateness of this ornamentation
throws light on the apostle Peter's counsel to Christian
women not to make their adornment external, e.g. the
braiding of the hair, the wearing of jewels of gold, the
putting on of showy apparel, but rather the apparel of a
meek and quiet spirit (1Pe_3:3, 1Pe_3:4).

7. Religious Devotion and Service:
The reflections cast upon women for her leadership in
the first transgression
(Gen_3:6, Gen_3:13, Gen_3:16; 2Co_11:3; 1Ti_2:14) do
not indicate her rightful and subsequent place in the
religious life of mankind. As wife, mother, sister, she has
been preeminently devout and spiritual. history records,
however, sad and striking exceptions to this rule.

Intertestamental Period

The women portrayed in the apocryphal literature of the
Jews reveal all the varied characteristics of their sex so
conspicuous in Tenach history: devout piety, ardent
patriotism, poetic fervor, political intrigue, worldly
ambition, and sometimes a strange combination of these
contradictory moral qualities. Whether fictitious, or
rounded on fact, or historical, these portrayals are true to
the feminine life of that era.

Anna is a beautiful example of wifely devotion. By her faith and hard toil she supported her husband, Tobit, after the loss of his property and in his blindness, until sight and prosperity were both restored (Tobit 1:9; 2:1-14).

Edna, wife of Raguel of Ecbatana and mother of Sarah, made her maternal love and piety conspicuous in the blessing bestowed on Tobias on the occasion of his marriage to her daughter, who had hitherto been cursed on the night of wedlock by the death of seven successive husbands (Tobit 7; 10:12).

Sarah, innocent of their death, which had been compassed by the evil spirit Asmodeus, at last had the reward of her faith in the joys of a happy marriage (Tobit 10:10; 14:13).

Judith, a rich young widow, celebrated in Hebrew lore as the savior of her nation, was devoutly and ardently patriotic. When Nebuchadnezzar sent his general Holofernes with an army of 132,000 men to subjugate the Jews, she felt called of God to be their deliverer. Visiting holofernes, she so captivated him with her beauty and gifts that he made a banquet in her honor. While he was excessively drunk with the wine of his own bounty, she beheaded him in his tent. The Assyrians, paralyzed by the loss of their leader, easily fell a prey to the armies of Israel. Judith celebrates her triumph in a song, akin in its triumphant joy, patriotic fervor and religious zeal, to the ancient songs of Miriam and Deborah (Judith 16:1-17).

Susanna typifies the ideal of womanly virtue. The daughter of righteous parents, well instructed in the sacred Law, the wife of a rich and honorable man, Joachim by name, she was richly blessed in position and person. Exceptionally modest, devout and withal very beautiful, she attracted the notice of two elders, who were also judges, and who took occasion frequently to visit Joachim's house. She spurned their advances and when falsely charged by them with the sin which she so successfully resisted, she escapes the judgment brought against her, by the subtle skill of Daniel. As a result, his fame and her innocence became widely known.

In Apostolic/New Testament Times

1. Miriam/Mary and Elisabeth:[47]
A new era dawned for women with the advent of Messiah Yeshua. The honor conferred upon Miriam/Mary, as mother of Jesus/Yeshua, lifted her from her "low estate," made after generations call her blessed (Lk_1:48), and carried its benediction to the women of all subsequent times. Lk's narrative of the birth of Messiah (Lk 1; 2) has thrown about motherhood the halo of a new sanctity, given mankind a more exalted conception of women's character and mission, and made the world's literature the vehicle of the same lofty reverence and regard. The two dispensations were

---

[47] Outline from ISBE=International Standard Bible Encyclopedia woman
http://www.internationalstandardbible.com/W/women.html

brought together in the persons of Elisabeth and Mary:
the former the mother of John the Baptist, the last of the
old order of prophets; the latter the mother of the long-
expected Messiah. Both are illustrious examples of
Spirit-guided and Spirit-filled womanhood. The story of
Mary's intellectual gifts, spiritual exaltation, purity and
beauty of character, and her training of her divine child,
has been an inestimable contribution to women's world-
wide emancipation, and to the uplift and ennoblement of
family life. To her poetic inspiration, spiritual fervor and
exalted thankfulness as expectant mother of the Messiah,
the church universal is indebted for its earliest and most
majestic hymn, the *Magnificat*. In her the religious
teachings, prophetic hopes, and noblest ideals of her race
were epitomized.

Jesus/Yeshua' reverence for women and the new respect
for her begotten by his teaching were well grounded, on
their human side, in the qualities of his own mother. The
fact that he himself was born of women has been cited to
her praise in the ecumenical creeds of Christendom.

It is obvious that Miriam/Mary was someone God could
absolutely trust with the precious gift of His Son that He
was sending into the World. We do not worship Miriam,
however she must have been a very special and spiritual
young woman, for God to choose her above all others.
She was a Torah Observant Jewish young woman who
would become a vessel mightily used by YHWH to
change the World via Yeshua HaMashiach.

2. Jesus/Yeshua and Women:[48]

From the first, women were responsive to his teachings
and devoted to his person. The sisters of
Lazarus, Mary and Martha, made their home at Bethany,
his dearest earthly refuge and resting-place. Women of
all ranks in society found in him a benefactor and friend,
before unknown in all the history of their sex. They
accompanied him, with the Twelve, in his preaching
tours from city to city, some, like Mary Magdalene,
grateful because healed of their moral infirmities
(Lk 8:2); others, like Joanna the wife of Chuzas,
and Susanna, to minister to his needs (Lk 8:3). Even
those who were ostracized by society were recognized
by him, on the basis of immortal values, and restored to
a womanhood of virtue and Christian devotion
(Lk 7:37-50). Mothers had occasion to rejoice in his
blessing their children (Mar 10:13-16); and in his
raising their dead (Lk 7:12-15). Women followed him
on his last journey from Galilee to Jerusalem; ministered
to Him on the way to Calvary (Mat 27:55, Mat 27:56);
witnessed his crucifixion (Lk 23:49); accompanied his
body to the sepulcher (Mat 27:61; Lk 23:55); prepared
spices and ointments for his burial (Lk 23:56); were first
at the tomb on the morning of his resurrection
(Mat 28:1; Mar 16:1; Lk 24:1; Joh 20:1); and were the
first to whom the risen Lord appeared
(Mat 28:9; Mar 16:9; Joh 20:14). Among those thus
faithful and favored were Mary Magdalene, Mary the

---

[48] Outline from ISBE=International Standard Bible Encyclopedia woman
http://www.internationalstandardbible.com/W/women.html

mother of James and Joses, Salome (Mat_27:56), Joanna and other unnamed women (Lk_24:10). Women had the honor of being the first to announce the fact of the resurrection to the chosen disciples (Lk_24:9, Lk_24:10, Lk_24:22). They, including the mother of Jesus/Yeshua, were among the 120 who continued in prayer in the upper room and received the Pentecostal endowment (Act_1:14); they were among the first Christian converts (Act_8:12); suffered equally with men in the early persecutions of the church (Act_9:2). The Jewish enemies of the new faith sought their aid and influence in the persecutions raised against Paul and Barnabas (Act_13:50); while women of equal rank among the Greeks became ardent and intelligent believers (Act_17:12). The fidelity of women to Jesus/Yeshua during his three years' ministry, and at the cross and sepulcher, typifies their spiritual devotion in the activities and enterprises of the church of the 20th century.

3. In the Early Kahilah/Church:[49]
Women were prominent, from the first, in the activities of the early church. Their faith and prayers helped to make Pentecost possible (Act_1:14). They were eminent, as in the case of Dorcas, in charity and good deeds (Act_9:36); foremost in prayer, like Mary the mother of John, who assembled the disciples at her home to pray for Peter's deliverance (Act_12:12). Priscilla is equally

---

[49] Outline from ISBE=International Standard Bible Encyclopedia woman
http://www.internationalstandardbible.com/W/women.html

gifted with her husband as an expounder of "the way of God," and instructor of Apollos (Act_18:26), and as Paul's "fellow-worker in Christ" (Rom_16:3).
The daughters of Philip were prophetesses
(Act_21:8, Act_21:9). The first convert in Europe was a woman, Lydia of Thyatira, whose hospitality made a home for Paul and a meeting-place for the infant church (Act_16:14). Women, as truly as men, were recipients of the charismatic gifts of Christianity. The apostolic greetings in the Epistles give them a place of honor. The church at Rome seems to have been blessed with a goodly number of gifted and consecrated women, inasmuch as Paul in the closing salutations of his Epistles sends greetings to at least eight prominent in Christian activity: Phoebe, Prisca, Mary "who bestowed much labor on
you," Tryphena and Tryphosa, Persis, Julia, and the sister of
Nereus (Rom_16:1,Rom_16:3, Rom_16:6, Rom_16:12, Rom_16:15). To no women did the great apostle feel himself more deeply indebted than to Lois and Eunice, grandmother and mother of Timothy, whose "faith unfeigned" and ceaseless instructions from the holy Scriptures (2Ti_1:5; 2Ti_3:14, 2Ti_3:15) gave him the most "beloved child" and assistant in his ministry. Their names have been conspicuous in Christian history for maternal love, spiritual devotion and fidelity in teaching the Word of God. See also CLAUDIA.

Many women preached and taught the BESORAH of Yeshua in the First Century. It is obvious that in the Apostolic Scriptures, women had an important role in

proclaiming the Good News of Salvation and that
Messiah has come.

4. Official Service:

From the first, women held official positions of influence
in the church. Phoebe (Rom_16:1) was evidently a
deaconess, whom Paul terms "a servant of the church,"
"a helper of many" and of himself also. Those women
who "labored with me in the gospel" (Phi_4:3)
undoubtedly participated with him in preaching. Later
on, the apostle used his authority to revoke this privilege,
possibly because some women had been offensively
forward in "usurping authority over the man"
(1Ti_2:12 the King James Version). Even though he
bases his argument for women's keeping silence in
public worship on Adam's priority of creation and her
priority in transgression (1Ti_2:13, 1Ti_2:14), modern
scholarship unhesitatingly affirms that his prohibition
was applicable only to the peculiar conditions of his own
time. Her culture, grace, scholarship, ability, religious
devotion and spiritual endowment make it evident that
she is often as truly called of God to public address and
instruction as man. It is evident in the New Testament
and in the writings of the Apostolic Fathers that women,
through the agency of two ecclesiastical orders, were
assigned official duties in the conduct and ministrations
of the early church.

Paul was not anti-women as many would try to
proclaim, in fact many women as stated above worked
with him in the ministry and reaching the Gentiles for
Yeshua.

5. Widows:[50]
Their existence as a distinct order is indicated
in 1Ti_5:9, 1Ti_5:10, where Paul directs Timothy as to
the conditions of their enrollment. No widow should be
"enrolled" (καταλέγω, *katalégō*, "catalogued,"
"registered") under 60 years of age, or if more than once
married. She must be "well reported of for good works";
a mother, having "brought up children"; hospitable,
having "used hospitality to strangers"; Christ like in
loving service, having "washed the saints' feet."
Chrysostom and Tertullian make mention of this order. It
bound its members to the service of God for life, and
assigned them ecclesiastical duties, e.g. the
superintendence of the rest of the women, and the charge
of the widows and orphans supported at public expense.
Dean Alford (see the Commentary in the place cited)
says they "were vowed to perpetual widowhood, clad in
a vestis vidualis ("widow's garments"), and ordained by
the laying on of hands. This institution was abolished by
the eleventh Canon of the council of Laodicea."

Other special duties, mentioned by the Church Fathers,
included prayer and fasting, visiting the sick, instruction
of women, preparing them for baptism, assisting in the
administration of this sacrament, and taking them the
communion. The spiritual nature of the office is
indicated by its occupant being variously termed "the

---

[50] Outline from ISBE=International Standard Bible Encyclopedia woman
http://www.internationalstandardbible.com/W/women.html

intercessor of the church"; "the keeper of the door," at
public service; "the altar of God." See WIDOWS.

6. Deaconesses:

Many of these duties were transferred, by the 3rd
century, to the deaconesses, an order which in recent
history has been restored to its original importance and
effectiveness. The women already referred to in
Rom_16:1, Rom_16:6, Rom_16:12 were evidently of
this order, the term διάκονος, *diákonos*, being
specifically applied to Phoebe, a deaconess of the church
at Cenchrea. The women of 1Ti_3:11, who were to serve
"in like manner" as the "deacons" of 1Ti_3:10,
presumably held this office, as also the "aged women"
of Tit_2:3 (= "presbyters"
(feminine), πρεσβύτεραι, *presbúterai*, 1Ti_5:2). Virgins
as well as widows were elected to this office, and the age
of eligibility was changed from 60 to 40 by the Council
of Chalcedon. The order was suppressed in the Latin
church in the 6th century, and in the Greek church in the
12th. because of certain abuses that gradually became
prevalent. Owing, however, to its exceptional importance
and value it has been reinstated by nearly all branches of
the modern church, the Methodists especially
emphasizing its spiritual efficiency. Special training
schools and courses in education now prepare candidates
for this office. Even as early as the Puritan Reformation
in England the Congregationalists recognized this order
of female workers in their discipline. The spiritual value
of women's ministry in the lay and official work of the
church is evidenced by her leadership in all branches of
ecclesiastical and missionary enterprise. This modern

estimate of her capability and place revises the entire
historic conception and attitude of mankind.

It seems that the prejudice against women in leadership
became more intense with the Church Fathers and going
forward in time from there.   There were always
exceptions to the rule regarding women in leadership,
but the majority took a dim view of women in the pulpit
or holding any leadership position which we will see
later. [51]

---

[51] Outline from ISBE=International Standard Bible Encyclopedia woman
http://www.internationalstandardbible.com/W/women.html

The Impact of Women in Their Home and their Unique Mission in Life

To impact our homes and families and the world we need to Keep a balance as woman of God.

I want to quote some nuggets from a wonderful book called; Women's Wisdom – The Garden of Peace for Woman – Rabbi Shalom Arush[52]

Marriage: Fulfilling Creation's Purpose pg 31

"The Torah says, "And God created man in His image; in the image of God He created him; male and female he created them" (Gen 1:27). This verse teaches that "man' refers to both male and female together. One without the other is not considered "man'. Hence, only a married man is called 'man", as it says in the Zohar that 'any image that does not depict both man and woman does not represent the Heavenly image of man. For the supernal image "His image' is both male and female. 'Therefore, when a genuine connection between man and woman is missing, a lack of love (Ahavah:" love" in the Holy Language, which is equivalent to Hebrew numerology to echad or "one") between man and wife, the Heavenly image of man is incomplete.

---

[52] Women's Wisdom – The Garden of Peace For Woman – Rabbi Shalom Arush Chut Shel Chessed Institutions, POB 50226 Jerusalem Israel www.meyemuna.com

This teaches us a basic law in spirituality; wherever there is no love between male and female, and no unity, the Holy One Blessed be He does not dwell. So even if a person is truly pious individual, if he is in a place where there is no unity between male and female...Hashem is not there."

The Midrash says that a man should not be without a wife, and a woman should not be without a husband, and the two should not be without God. We learn from here that a man without a wife is nothing. Conversely, a woman without a husband is nothing. Together, they are nothing without Hashem. Without peace in our home, they do not merit the Divine Presence, the Shechina, and without the Divine Presence they are as nothing. The Divine Presence only dwells in a home where there is peace and harmony between man and wife"

We see in God's eyes man and woman are one, equal but as we have seen different. Men and Women need each other to be a complete unit. What one lacks, the other makes up for, or compliments. That is why at times, when our roles are confused there will be conflict, or when we do not allow each other to function in our gifts that God put within us, there will also be conflict.

What about woman who are single or widows, are they cast aside and nothing? No, God has taken care of that by being a husband to the woman who is not married.

Isa 54:1 "Sing, O barren one, who did not bear; break forth into singing and cry aloud, you who have not been in labor! For the children of the desolate one will be more than the children of her who is married," says the LORD.

Isa 54:2 "Enlarge the place of your tent, and let the curtains of your habitations be stretched out; do not hold back; lengthen your cords and strengthen your stakes.

Isa 54:3 For you will spread abroad to the right and to the left, and your offspring will possess the nations and will people the desolate cities.

Isa 54:4 "Fear not, for you will not be ashamed; be not confounded, for you will not be disgraced; for you will forget the shame of your youth, and the reproach of your widowhood you will remember no more.

Isa 54:5 For your Maker is your husband, the LORD of hosts is his name; and the Holy One of Israel is your Redeemer, the God of the whole earth he is called.

Isa 54:6 For the LORD has called you like a wife deserted and grieved in spirit, like a wife of youth when she is cast off, says your God.

Isa 54:7 For a brief moment I deserted you, but with great compassion I will gather you.

Isa 54:8 In overflowing anger for a moment I hid my face from you, but with everlasting love I will have compassion on you," says the LORD, your Redeemer.

Isa 54:9 "This is like the days of Noah to me: as I swore that the waters of Noah should no more go over the earth, so I have sworn that I will not be angry with you, and will not rebuke you.

Isa 54:10 For the mountains may depart and the hills be removed, but my steadfast love shall not depart from

you, and my covenant of peace shall not be removed,"
says the LORD, who has compassion on you.

Isa 54:11 "O afflicted one, storm-tossed and not
comforted, behold, I will set your stones in antimony,
and lay your foundations with sapphires.

Isa 54:12 I will make your pinnacles of agate, your gates
of carbuncles, and all your wall of precious stones.

Isa 54:13 All your children shall be taught by the
LORD, and great shall be the peace of your children.

Isa 54:14 In righteousness you shall be established; you
shall be far from oppression, for you shall not fear; and
from terror, for it shall not come near you.

Isa 54:15 If anyone stirs up strife, it is not from me;
whoever stirs up strife with you shall fall because of
you.

Isa 54:16 Behold, I have created the smith who blows
the fire of coals and produces a weapon for its purpose. I
have also created the ravager to destroy;

Isa 54:17 no weapon that is fashioned against you shall
succeed, and you shall refute every tongue that rises
against you in judgment. This is the heritage of the
servants of the LORD and their vindication from me,
declares the LORD." (ESV)

Yes, this is talking about Israel, but I believe it is also a
word of comfort to those who are single as well. We
God, we are never alone or forsaken. God has used
many single woman in a great way, for example Corrie
Ten Boom to name one.

Motherhood pg. 226[53]

"One of the most vital and praiseworthy facets of being a woman is raising children. There is nothing greater than a mother and educator who builds her home and literally ensures the future of mankind on this planet.

Many women approach motherhood with some disdain ad apprehension. You only have to think about what motherhood entails to understand why: screaming babies, dirty diapers, sibling rivalry, problems at school, issues with friends, teenage growing pains and rebelliousness, health problems, God forbid the list is long."

Those of us who are mothers and have raised our children to fear God, the greatest reward we could ask in this life is to see them serving Him. However, there have been many broken hearts in mothers, when their children choose to walk a different path other than God has called them to. However, our prayers as mothers are powerful and the Word that has been sown in tears, I believe we will reap in joy when the Prodigals come home.

When you see football players or other athletes in front of the cameras who do the majority of them acknowledge, their moms! Yes, fathers have an impact as well, but mom is the heart and soul of the home. As

---

[53] Wisdom of Woman – The Garden of Peace For Woman – Rabbi Shalom Arush Chut Shel Chessed Institutions, POB 50226 Jerusalem Israel www.meyemuna.com

we have shown early, there is a special connection
between mother and child from the womb.

As mothers, we have a unique opportunity to impact our
children in all areas of their lives, but especially when it
comes to their relationship with God.

Women's Unique Mission pg. 311[54]

"Woman have a unique and wonderful mission in this
world. Our sages teach that by virtue of our righteous
woman, we were redeemed from Egypt; thanks to our
righteous women, we will also merit the final
redemption of our people.

Woman are on a lofty spiritual level. They have an
elevated capacity for developing emuna and accepting
Divine Providence. In the Morning Benedictions, they
merit to say things that e3ven the greatest tsaddikim
can't say; "Thank God I have been created according to
His Will." This blessing expresses the genuine aspiration
of a true servant of God. True servants of Hashem year
to nullify their own wants and desires to the level where
they are only wish tis be exactly like Hashem wants
them to be. Women inherently want to be what Hashem
wants them to be, so every morning they thank Hashem
for making them that way.

---

[54] Wisdom of Woman – The Garden of Peace For Woman – Rabbi Shalom
Arush Chut Shel Chessed Institutions, POB 50226 Jerusalem Israel
www.meyemuna.com

Give their unique and lofty mission, women must
continually work on improving their character traits,
their prayers, their faith, and their Torah learning.
Although women spend less time than men on "purely"
spiritual mitzvoth like wearing tefillin or learning Torah,
their faith and character are constantly being tested in the
home."

Now this is from a Rabbinical point of view, because I
would venture to say that many spiritual women
probably spend as much or even more time in the Word
in study and in prayer.

A Woman's Prayer pg. 318[55]

Our patriarchs, matriarchs and all the righteous men and
woman throughout the generations devoted extensive
time to prayer-especially personal payer. Abraham, Isaac,
Jacob, Sarah, Rebecca, Rachel and Leah all prayed. The
Torah cites the prayers of Moses on many different
occasion. Chana prayed for a child subsequently gave
birth to Samuel, who in turn led the people of Israel.
King David testified about himself, "I am prayer-he
wrote in the book of Psalms, which is only a partial
compendium of his endless prayers.

After the destruction of our Holy Temples, the tradition
of prayer and hitbodedut continued with Mordehai and

---

[55] Wisdom of Woman – The Garden of Peace For Woman – Rabbi Shalom
Arush Chut Shel Chessed Institutions, POB 50226 Jerusalem Israel
www.meyemuna.com

Queen Esther, and closer to our times, with the Holy Ball Shem Tov and Rebbe Nachman of Breslev, just to name but a few. All our righteous beacons of spirituality spent a great deal of time praying.

The Torah tells many stories of righteous women who busied themselves with prayer day and night. Our Talmudic sages teach (*Gemara Magillah 14*) that Sarah's level of prophecy was even greater than Abraham's' "Rabbi Isaac said" Yiscah is Sara; and why was she called Yiscah? Because she was anointed ('*saketha*') with holy spirit, as the Torah says "Whatever Sara tells you; hearken to her voice" (*Genesis 221:12*).

Hashem could have instructed Abraham to just listen to Sarah when it came to Yishmael. However, He told Abraham to list to her in all matters. Our sages hereby learn that Sarah's level of prophecy was greater than Abraham's.

Our other matriarchs were also blessed with the gift of prophecy and the ability to perform miracles-they would light the Sabbath Candles and their candles would stay lit all week, the Divine Presence dwelt in their tents;' and the well water would rise up toward them in a way to make I easier for them to draw water from the well. In order to reach such lofty levels, these righteous women were constantly busy in the service of God.

A Woman's Greatness pg. 379

Our sages teach (*Gemara, Shabbat 62*) that women are
like a "separate nation". They have certain positive
character traits that most men lack.

Women are the most unique of God's creations. Hashem
created women when he saw that men could not thrive
on their own, as the Torah says: "And the Lord God said,
"It is not good that man is alone; I shall make him a
helpmate opposite him" (*Genesis 2:18*) Hashem created
woman as a helpmate for men, for only through the help
of his wife can a man attain his true mission in life. The
woman's role as her husband's helpmate is consequently
of unique importance.

A Woman's Superiority pg.388[56]

When it comes to spirituality, women usually start off at
a much higher point then men, since men have a much
greater Evil Inclination.

Page 389 A woman's imagination is more purified than a
man's. Therefore, her Evil Inclination is smaller than his.
A woman can achieve a much higher spiritual level with
much less effort than a man can. A woman's Evil
Inclination focuses predominantly on speech and the

---

[56] Wisdom of Woman – The Garden of Peace For Woman – Rabbi Shalom
Arush Chut Shel Chessed Institutions, POB 50226 Jerusalem Israel
www.meyemuna.com

mouth. Therefore, if she guards her tongue, she can truly
reach very high spiritual levels.

Jewish Women's Impact in The Past – Ancient Records

In my researching, I found resources showing the impact of Jewish Women in the Ancient Near East. Far from being sub-servient and only keepers of their home, we find that some were involved in commerce and even in Synagogue leadership and were highly respected among their peers.

Here are some examples from history from JPS Guide to Jewish Women, this is not a comprehensive list but only a sampling of various Jewish women who lived in the ANE:

BIOGRAPHIES[57]

BABATHA OF MAHOZA, PROPERTY OWNER
(2nd century C.E.)
Babatha, a woman of property, is known only through a cache of thirty-five papyrus documents found in 1961 in a cave in the Judean desert. From these documents, we know that she engaged in business and litigation regarding her own interests and those of her son. She lived in Mahoza, a town on the southern end of the Dead Sea, in the Nabatean region of the land of Israel.

---

[57] Taitz, E., Henry, S., & Tallan, C. (2003). *The JPS Guide to Jewish Women: 600 B.C.E–1900 C.E.* Philadelphia: The Jewish Publication Society

Babatha's second husband was Judah ben Eleazer Khtusion of Ein-Gedi. He died three years after the wedding, bequeathing to Babatha considerable property. In 131 C.E. members of Judah's family, including a first wife, Miriam, contested the will. The determination of this suit is not known, but Babatha did have to hand over some property to Khtusion's family.

As a widow, Babatha remained involved in the business and legal affairs of her stepdaughter, Shelamzion. This may have been the result of a loan made to her husband for Shelamzion's dowry that was not yet repaid at the time of Judah's death.

Whether Babatha survived the Bar Kokhba rebellion or its aftermath is not known.

MIBTAHIAH OF ELEPHANTINE, PROPERTY OWNER

(5th century B.C.E.)
Mibtahiah was a prosperous woman who lived on Elephantine, a small island in the Nile River with a thriving Jewish community. Born in 476 B.C.E. to a well-to-do family that owned property and slaves, the meager facts of her life are contained in eleven papyri, discovered by diggers near Aswan, Egypt. These documents, written in Aramaic, clearly show the amount of property Mibtahiah owned and how it was legally protected.

Mibtahiah had two brothers, Gemariah and Jedaniah. Probably in order to bypass the biblical ruling that

daughters cannot inherit if there are sons, her father,
Mahseiah, gifted property to her at the time of her
marriages.

Mibtahiah's first husband was Jezaniah, the Jew who
owned the plot of land next to her father's house. The
marriage, which took place in 460 or 459 B.C.E. when she
was approximately sixteen years old, was marked by two
transfers of a deed for a building plot: one by Mahseiah to
his daughter, granting her title to the property, and the
second to Jezaniah giving him the income only. This was
a typical dowry arrangement at that time. Jezaniah died
shortly after the marriage, and there was no record of any
children.

Eshor the Egyptian was Mibtahiah's second husband,
whom she married in 449 B.C.E. For this marriage there is
an existing contract called a "document of wifehood,"
stipulating that either party could initiate divorce, a right
that was not common to Jewish women in later periods.

The union of Mibtahiah and Eshor produced two sons,
Jedaniah and Mahseiah. When Mibtahiah died in 416
B.C.E. at the age of sixty-four, she left a considerable estate
to her sons, including both real and personal property.

Mibtahiah emerges as a woman who had considerable
control over her own life. She was guaranteed status as an
only wife, was free to divorce at will, and acted
independently in business.

RUFINA OF SMYRNA, HEAD OF A SYNAGOGUE
(2nd century C.E.)
Rufina was an established and respected citizen of
Smyrna (Turkey) who owned property and slaves. She is
known only by an inscription on a tombstone that she had
built for her freed slaves. This inscription specifically
identifies her as a Jew and head of a synagogue
(archisynagogissa). Hers is one of nineteen Greek and
Latin inscriptions referring to Jewish women in the
Mediterranean area over several centuries.[23] Many of
them were listed as "head of synagogue."

The inscription contains a threat to impose a fine on any
person who dares to bury another body in that spot. The
proceeds of the fine were to be split between the Jewish
community and the "sacred treasury" (possibly the
Imperial treasury or the treasury of a pagan temple,
suggesting that Rufina may have been a convert from
paganism). The fact that a copy of this warning was filed
in the public archives indicates that Rufina was an
influential woman. There is no mention of a husband and
no evidence that her title was derived from a husband or
other male relative.

**SHELAMZION OF SOUTHERN ISRAEL,
PROPERTY OWNER**
(2nd century C.E.)
Shelamzion was the daughter of Judah Khtusion and
Miriam. Her marriage contract and other documents
concerning her were found, together with documents
belonging to her stepmother, Babatha, in the Cave of
Letters in the Judean Desert.

These papers, undoubtedly placed there for safekeeping during the Bar Kokhba rebellion, reveal a few facts about Shelamzion's life. Her marriage contract with Judah Cimber, written in Greek, followed Hellenistic rather than Jewish law. The dowry stipulated in the contract included silver, gold, and clothing. There was a promised future payment of three hundred dinars by Judah to Shelamzion.

Shelamzion also owned property in her own name, deeded to her by her father eleven days after her wedding. Her wedding dowry may have been secured by means of a loan   from   Babatha   to   her   father.

SOPHIA OF GORTYN, HEAD OF A SYNAGOGUE
(4th or 5th century C.E.)
Only Sophia's tombstone, found in Kastelli, Kissamou, on the island of Crete, marks her as "elder and head of the synagogue." As is the case with Rufina, there is no mention of a husband, nor any reason to assume that her title was derived from him as some historians have suggested.

TAMET OF ELEPHANTINE, FORMER SLAVE
(5th century B.C.E.)
According to documentation from the Elephantine papyri, Tamet was the slave of Meshullam ben Zaccur. Her status, translated as "handmaid," changed when Meshullam gave her in marriage to Ananiah, son of Azariah. Although she received no bride-price, she came to her husband with a small dowry, probably provided by her former master. Her marriage contract explicitly grants her the right of divorce,

indicating that this right was common in Elephantine and
not merely a privilege of rich women.

Tamet and Ananiah had at least one child, a daughter
Jehoishma whose marriage contract was also found
among the Elephantine papyri.

THEOPEMTE OF MYNDOS, PHILANTHROPIST
(4th, 5th, or 6th century C.E.)
Theopemte lived in Myndos, Caria, a district on the
southwest coast of Asia Minor. Her large donation to the
synagogue, given together with her son Eusebios, was
acknowledged on a white marble post retrieved from the
ruins in that area. The inscription, tentatively dated from
the sixth century, names her as head of the synagogue.

THE WORLD OF JEWISH WOMEN IN
ECONOMIC ACTIVITIES
Most archeological evidence relating to the economic
activities of Jewish women in this early period teaches us
about women who were prosperous. Because deeds,
donations, and ownership lists were most often what was
recorded in ancient societies, it is this kind of information
that remains. Such records, preserved either in stone or on
papyrus, reveal women as property owners,
philanthropists, and buyers and sellers of real estate or
large amounts of movable goods. Some women owned
herds of livestock, either alone or together with a husband.

EDUCATION
Archeological evidence in the form of scrolls and other
ancient documents casts little light on how Jewish women

were educated. Rich women, or those from learned families, were certainly taught more than those from peasant families, where the education of men was also limited. Records such as deeds and contracts may indicate little more than the fact that a woman could sign her name.

PUBLIC POWER

While women may have had a certain amount of power in the home, public power was traditionally closed to them from earliest times. For this reason, any tangible evidence of women who held some form of official rank or influence, no matter how minor, is noteworthy. This is the case for the most recent discovery of seals dating from the pre-exilic and postexilic Jewish kingdoms.

For the most part, only royal officials or their deputies—people who held power—possessed seals. For this reason, it was particularly intriguing to discover, among a hoard of such seals, thirteen that belonged to women. Most of these thirteen seals identify the women merely as "daughter of" or "wife of," as for example "Abigayil, wife of Asayahu," or "Yeho'adan, daughter of Uriyahu." A few give names that have been connected with the ruling families of Judea, although not all are from royal families.

An interesting seal found together with a collection of official documents names the owner as "Shelomit maidservant of Elnatan the governor."[63] The meaning of the word "maidservant" is not clear in this context. It may have been used as the female equivalent of servant (*eved*) to designate a high official, or it may have meant the governor's wife. In either case, it is assumed that she held an appointed position of some import in Judea.

Other hints that a few women enjoyed some form of public power many centuries later have also been uncovered. These are in the form of nineteen Greek and Latin inscriptions written in stone and dating from 27 B.C.E. to the sixth century C.E. These inscriptions were found in areas extending from Italy to Turkey, Egypt, and the land of Israel and include women's names and titles. Notable among the titles are "head of the synagogue" (archisynagogissa), "elder," "leader," and "mother of the synagogue."

Until recently, historians and archeologists have dismissed such labels as honorific, assuming that women could not possibly have held positions of leadership in ancient synagogues or Jewish communities. In the last decades of the twentieth century, however, women scholars began to challenge those old opinions.[64] They claim that there is no evidence from ancient Judaism that wives or widows routinely took on their husbands' titles. Their continuing investigations suggest that women such as Rufina of Smyrna, Sophia of Gortyn and Theopempte of Caria, all holding the title of archisynagogissa, were important functionaries in the Jewish community.

When the archisynagogue title applied to men, the position assumed wealth. The men were usually from families of high status and were responsible for assigning people to the reading of the law, inviting preachers to the synagogue, and collecting money from the congregation for synagogue building and restoration. There seems no reason that women holding that title in their own right would not have done the same. While their administrative and fund-raising duties may have been directed especially to the women, there was no clear sign indicating that even this was so.

RELIGIOUS PARTICIPATION
Involvement in Synagogues

As early as the fifth century B.C.E., there is evidence that women were involved in religious life. Lists of contributors to the Jewish Temple in Elephantine make it clear that many women made regular donations in their own names. These women were financially independent and had the legal right to dispose of their own money and goods.

Centuries later, the engravings on stone monuments found in Mediterranean lands attest to similar participation by women both as donors and lay leaders. In the eastern Mediterranean region, Sophia of Gortyn (4th or 5th century C.E.) was an elder (*presbytera*) in her synagogue as well as an archisynagogissa. Several other examples of women with the title of "elder" have been recorded in the early centuries of the Common Era. These include Rebekka of Thrace, Beronikene of Thessaly, and Mannine of Italy. Peristeria of Thessaly is referred to as "leader."

Veturia Paulla (date unknown) held the title "mother of the synagogue" for two separate synagogues in Rome. While this title may have been honorary, it most probably was accorded to women (and men) who gave sizable donations. Veturia Paulla was a gentile who converted to Judaism at the age of seventy.[6]

Tation and Theopemte had no religious titles, but they too were generous donors to synagogues. The same can be assumed for the nine women whose names are preserved on the mosaic floor of a synagogue in Apamea, Syria. Other women's names also appear as benefactors in that same mosaic, but they are listed in groups together with men, so they may not have controlled their own money.

Such inscriptions—and there may be more as yet undiscovered—stand in stark contrast to written rabbinic sources that claim women should be secluded and were uninvolved in the activities of the synagogue or the study hall. However, these inscriptions do not suggest that women were prayer leaders, either. Nor do they show that women were active in any of the ritual activities that rabbinic law demanded of men. The Greek inscriptions referring to a few Jewish women (Marin from lower Egypt, Gaudentia of Rome, and Lady Maria of Beth She'arim) as "priest" (*hierissa*),[70] describe no specific religious function.

Women's treatment and status under Islam; The following is from the Website "What Makes Islam so Different"

Wherever Islam takes over, woman suffer greatly. They are treated like property, murdered, sold as slaves and treated as personal property. Woman who have escaped Islam have described atrocities beyond our civilized understanding. Abuse of woman under Isalm includes, genital mutilation, honor killings, rape, child marriages, multiple spouses, beatings, all that are considered legal under Sharia law.

A woman's Worth per The Quran

Quran (4:11) - (Inheritance) "The male shall have the equal of the portion of two females" (see also verse 4:176). In Islam, sexism is mathematically established.

Quran (2:282) - (Court testimony) "And call to witness, from among your men, two witnesses. And if two men be not found then a man and two women." Muslim apologists offer creative explanations to explain why Allah felt that a man's testimony in court should be valued twice as highly as a woman's, but studies consistently show that women are actually less likely to tell lies than men, meaning that they make more reliable witnesses.

Quran (2:228) - "and the men are a degree above them [women]"

Quran (5:6) - "And if ye are unclean, purify yourselves. And if ye are sick or on a journey, or one of you cometh from the closet, or ye have had contact with women, and ye find not water, then go to clean, high ground and rub your faces and your hands with some of it" Men are to rub dirt on their hands, if there is no water to purify them, following casual contact with a woman (such as shaking hands).

Quran (24:31) - Women are to lower their gaze around
men, so they do not look them in the eye. (To be fair,
men are told to do the same thing in the prior verse).

Quran (2:223) - "Your wives are as a tilth unto you; so
approach your tilth when or how ye will..." A man has
dominion over his wives' bodies as he does his land. This
verse is overtly sexual. There is some dispute as to
whether it is referring to the practice of anal intercourse.
If this is what Muhammad meant, then it would appear
to contradict what he said in Muslim (8:3365).

Quran (4:3) - (Wife-to-husband ratio) "Marry women of
your choice, Two or three or four" Inequality by
numbers.

Quran (53:27) - "Those who believe not in the Hereafter,
name the angels with female names." Angels are sublime
beings, and would therefore be male.

Quran (4:24) and Quran (33:50) - A man is permitted to
take women as sex slaves outside of marriage. Note that
the verse distinguishes wives from captives (those whom
they right hand possesses).

The move to paint Islam as a pioneering force in
women's rights is a recent one, corresponding with the
efforts of Muslim apologists (not otherwise known for
their feminist leanings) and some Western academics
prone to interpreting history according to personal
preference. In truth, the Islamic religious community has

never exhibited an interest in expanding opportunities
for women beyond the family role.

The fourth Caliph, who was Muhammad's son-in-law
and cousin, said just a few years after the prophet's death
that "The entire women is an evil. And what is worse is
that it is a necessary evil."

A traditional Islamic saying is that, "A woman's heaven
is beneath her husband's feet." One of the world's most
respected Quran commentaries explains that, "Women
are like cows, horses, and camels, for all are ridden."
(Tafsir al-Qurtubi)

The revered Islamic scholar, al-Ghazali, who has been
called 'the greatest Muslim after Muhammad,' writes that
the role of a Muslim women is to "stay at home and get
on with her sewing. She should not go out often, she
must not be well-informed, nor must she be
communicative with her neighbors and only visit them
when absolutely necessary; she should take care of her
husband... and seek to satisfy him in everything... Her
sole worry should be her virtue... She should be clean
and ready to satisfy her husband's sexual needs at any
moment." [Ibn Warraq]

A Yemeni cleric recently explained in a television
broadcast what makes women inferior and unable, say, to
serve as good witnesses: "Women are subject to
menstruation, when their endurance and mental capacity
for concentration are diminished. When a woman
witnesses a killing or an accident, she becomes

frightened, moves away, and sometimes even faints, and she cannot even watch the incident."

During a 2012 talk show on an Egyptian television channel, a cleric slammed Christianity - in part for teaching gender equality: "the Christian religion does not differentiate between women and men, but it confirms their perfect equality: it gives them an equal share in inheritance, it bans divorce, and it bans polygamy."

In 2014, Turkish President Recep Tayyip Erdogan emphasized that men and women are not equal: "Our religion has defined a position for women (in society): motherhood."

The many opportunities denied women under Islamic law, from equal testimony in court to the simple right to exclude other wives from their marital bed, is very clear proof that women are of lesser value then men in Islam. Muslim women are not even free to marry outside the faith - and some pay with their lives for doing so.

Islamic law also specifies that when a woman is murdered by a man, her family is owed only half as much "blood money" (diya) as they would be if she had been a man. (The life of a non-Muslim is generally assessed at one-third).

Although a man retains custody of his children in the event of his wife's death, a non-Muslim women will automatically lose custody of her children in the event of

her husband's death unless she converts to Islam or
marries a male relative within his family.

Contemporary Muslims like to counter that Arabs treated
women as camels prior to Muhammad. This is somewhat
questionable, given that Muhammad's first wife was a
wealthy women who owned property and ran a
successful business prior to ever meeting him. She was
even his boss... (although that may have changed after
the marriage). Still, it is somewhat telling that Islam's
treatment of women can only be defended by contrasting
it to an extremely primitive environment in which
women were said to be non-entities.

Homa Darabi was a talented physician who took her own
life by setting herself on fire in a public protest against
the oppression of women in Islamic Iran. She did this
after a 16-year-old girl was shot to death for wearing
lipstick. In the book, Why We Left Islam, her sister
includes a direct quote from one of the country's leading
clerics:

"The specific task of women in this society is to marry
and bear children. They will be discouraged from
entering legislative, judicial, or whatever careers which
may require decision-making, as women lack the
intellectual ability and discerning judgment required for
these careers."

Modern day cleric Abu Ishaq al-Huwaini has called for a
return of the slave markets, where Muslim men can order
concubines. In this man's ideal world, "when I want a

sex-slave, I go to the market and pick whichever female
I desire and buy her."
http://thereligionofpeace.com/pages/quran/women-
worth-less.aspx

At best, Islam "elevates" the status of a woman to
somewhere between that of a camel and a man.
Muhammad captured women in war and treated them as
a tradable commodity. The "immutable, ever-relevant"
Quran explicitly permits women to be kept as sex slaves.
These are hardly things in which Muslims can take pride.

Women's Impact in Leadership Positions

For many of us who have been called to be Leaders,
Rabbis and Teachers in the Body of Messiah, it has been
a long hard road. Many years of what could have been
fruitful ministry was hindered due to the prejudice
against women in Ministry. We have been falsely
accused and treated as if we had "bird brains" or have
been labeled "Feminists" which is farthest from the truth
for most of us.

Understanding a woman's role in spiritual leadership
must be built on the Tanakh foundation. Holy Scriptures
clearly define God's rules of female leadership.
Leadership roles in the believing community should be
aligned with Biblical patterns. While the Biblical pattern
clearly shows male predominance in leadership, it also
clearly shows female participation. Many women have
been anointed by the Holy Spirit/Ruach HaKodesh to fill
leadership roles..

When the call of God is burning in your heart, and others
continue to try to douse that fire, it can wear you out.
How many women could have made a great impact on
their generations, if only they were allowed to obey God
in their gifts and callings?

Form his book "10 Lies The Church Tells Women" J.
Lee Grady lists 10   reasons Churches have given to
women being restricted from leadership, and my
response. We will see that this is far from the truth in the

1st Century and even latter and that Paul was in no way anti-women.

Lie #1 – God created women as inferior beings, destined to serve their husbands

Yes women do not have the physical strength of a man, however what they do not have in physical strength, in many ways are superior in spiritual strength. Men and Women need one another, because what Adam lacked, Eve completed. Gen. 3

Lie#2 - Women are not equipped to assume leadership roles in the church

We have seen previously that God used women in many roles, and some were in the position of leadership, deliverers and even warriors

Lie #3 – Women must not teach or preach to men in a church setting

Deborah was a judge of Israel and men and women came to her for Torah rulings, and yes teaching!

Lie #4 – A woman should view her husband as the "priest of the home"

Yes, I agree our husbands are priests and should be respected as such, but we are also co laborers in Messiah

Lie #5 – A man needs to "cover" a woman in her ministry activities

Who God calls, God covers. Many great women of God were single and never married yet God used them in a great way, example Corrie Ten Boom

Lie #6 Women who exhibit strong leadership qualities pose a serious danger to the church
Many times we have been wrongly accused of having a "Jezebel" spirit because we have the ability of leadership. However the gifts and callings are from God and He is the one who gives certain women the ability to be leaders.

Lie #7 – Women are more easily deceived than men
Women tend to be more intuitive spiritually, men and women are equally open to being deceived if they do not pray and seek God. Many times, a woman will pick up on deception before her husband and help him in these areas, as a good help meet should.

Lie #8 Women can't be fulfilled or spiritually effective without a husband and children
Being a wife and mother is wonderful and yes fulfilling, but our ultimate fulfillment must come from our relationship with God whether we are married or single.

Lie #9 Women shouldn't work outside the home
In a perfect world, I am sure most women would rather not have to work outside the home. However, in today's world many women are forced into the work force out of financial necessity due to divorce, widowhood or not being able to make ends meet on one income. Some do this by choice and are able to balance work and family with no problem, but we see in the Bible many women of God were business women as well.

Lie #10 – Women must obediently submit to their husbands in all situations

If a husband is not saved or serving God a Godly women does not have to submit to anything that will cause her to break God's commandments or are contrary to living according to the Word or do things that are contrary to her moral conscience. If he is a God-fearing man, then he will see his wife as a helpmeet and himself as her protector and will never ask her to do something that will affect her relationship with the Father.

Lenore Lindsey Mullican makes the following points. [iv]

In her study of the role of women in the Old Testament period Rachel 0. Levine writes that women "was respected, her personhood was equivalent to that of a man, and she was considered to be a co-worker with the Lord in the creation of new life."8 Gretchen Hull's study concludes that the variety of women's functions included a single woman leader (Miriam), a resistance leader (Rahab), a good soldier (Jael), and a spiritual as well as judicial leader (Deborah) who was also a wife and mother.9

Although the primary role of the Jewish women in the first century was that of wife and mother, this was considered a position of prestige and honor and "in no way was she looked upon as being inferior to man."10 In studying rabbinic's it is necessary to realize that the Talmud was written over a wide span of time and reflected varying cultural and social situations; therefore,

the opinions therein differ.11 There are numerous
examples both in literature and in archeological findings,
however, of women in positions of leadership during the
first century B.C.E. and the first two centuries C.E.

There was a high regard for education and the mother
had the responsibility for the education of both boys and
girls in the primary years. Rabbinic writings show that
several women were considered scholars. These include
Ima Shalom (wife of Rabbi Eliezer Ben Hyrcanus, the
sister of Rabbi Gamaliel II); and Beruria (wife of Rabbi
Meir and daughter of Rabbi Haninah Ben Teradyon).
Beruria even contributed important halachic
decisions.12 The Talmud says concerning her that she
"studied three hundred laws from three hundred teachers
in [one] day."13

Talmud translator Rabbi H. Freedman states:

This is undoubtedly an exaggeration, but it is interesting
to note that a woman is cited as an illustration of wide
scholarship, thus showing that the Rabbis were by no
means averse to women studying as has been commonly
supposed.14

Due to her responsibilities, the women was exempt from
positive commands, the observances of which "depend
upon definite point of time."15 The demands of
motherhood took precedence over religious observances
outside the home; therefore, while permitted these
religious observances she was not required to do them as
was the man. This is the context of the benediction

recited daily by men: "a man is obliged to offer three benedictions daily: that He has made me an Israelite, that He has not made me a woman, that He has not made me a bore."16 The underlying motive is that of gratefulness for the privilege of "having the duty of carrying out the precepts of the law."17 This in no way implied a "degradation of women."18

Concerning the role of women in the temple, Shmuel Safrai states:

According to Jewish religious law, women were allowed in every area of the Temple precincts in which men were. The Mishnah specifies areas within the Temple which non-priests were allowed to enter, but it does not differentiate between men and women.19

Women had the privilege of participating in activities of the Temple. They were present for the three benedictions recited with the people following the daily preparation of the morning tamid.20 Also, women of priestly lineage had certain obligations just as the men did of bringing sacrifices and offerings to the Temple.21

The role of women in the synagogue has been reevaluated recently with the discovery that in the excavations of first century synagogues no evidence has been found for a separate women's gallery.22 In fact "all archaeological evidence points to just the opposite—a common meeting room for both men and women."23 No longer can we conclude that women were spectators but rather that they were actively involved in all aspects of the worship."v

The context of some rabbinic sources presupposes the
presence of women in synagogue services. The Mishnah
even ''provided that a woman could be one of the seven
called each Sabbath to publicly read from the Torah
scroll."24 Women were obligated to pray, according to
the Mishnah, "they are not exempt from saying
the Tefillah, from the law of the Mezuzah or from saying
the Benediction after meals."25 Although the issue was
related to distance walked to attend synagogue, the
following quote demonstrates the presupposition that
women attended synagogue to pray.

A certain widow had a synagogue in her neighborhood;
yet she used to come daily to the school of R. Johanan
and pray there. He said to her, "My daughter, is there not
a synagogue in your neighborhood?" She answered him,
"Rabbi, but have I not the reward for the steps!26
Archaeological studies have shown that women served
in many capacities in the synagogue. There are
numerous inscriptional evidences of women donors to
the synagogue and the honor they were given.27 That
Jewish women served in leadership positions is evident
from inscriptions denoting these functions. Bernadette
Brooten has made an extensive study of archeological
inscriptions and has noted evidence for such leadership
roles among women as:

1. Head of synagogue: archisynagogos, whose function
was in administration and exhortation.
2. Leader: archegissa, derived from archegos.

3. Elder: presbytera, with no indication that they were
the wives of elders; may have been involved in financial
oversight of the synagogue and/or have been scholars.
4. Mother of the Synagogue: meter synagoges, from
second century C.E. and later; their function may have
had to do with administration.
5. Members of Priestly Class: hiereia/hierissa, perhaps
equivalent to the rabbinic cohenet.28

**In the Book" Sacred Calling Four Decades of Women
in The Rabbinate"**

"Women have been rabbis for over forty years. The
Sacred Calling is about how our congregations, our
Jewish world and even our collective identity as Jews
have been revolutionized by the ordination of women in
the rabbinate. No longer are women rabbis a unique
phenomenon; rather, they have become an integral part
of the fabric of Jewish life."

In the Messianic Movement, we are still a little behind
our Jewish counterparts. In fact, the term "Rabbi" alone
is many times maligned and treated with disrespect, let
alone a woman carrying the title of "Rabbi", but we must
continue to persevere and be faithful and be examples of
Godly Women who bring glory to God in everything we
say in do, in our homes and outside of our homes as
well.

So what are some reasons that we can give for Women
Rabbis, Teachers and Leaders

DAUGHTERS OF ISRAEL AND THEIR IMPACT IN GODS
KINGDOM PAST, PRESENT AND FUTURE

#1. In the Gospels/Besorah we read of several women messengers who "proclaimed the Besorah/Good News – Matthew 28:1-10, Lk 24:9-11

#2. In Acts 2:14-21, Joel 2: 28-31 God predicted and promised that He Himself would pour out His Spirit/Ruach upon women and they would prophesy. To prophesy means to "speak to men to edification, exhortation and comfort" (1 Cor. 14:30)   to Edify the Assembly of Adonai (1 Cor. 14:4), Prophesying for the Assembly and general public. 1 Cor. 12:1-31, 1 Cor 14:1-6, 12, 24-26, 29-33

#3. In Acts 21:8-9 it is clear that Phillips 4 daughters were prophetesses, that is, they were evangelists like their father. This is in perfect accord with Joel 2:28-29 which was fulfilled in the early Kahilah (Acts. 2:16) and with Acts 2:17-18 which will be fulfilled in the last days.

#4. In Romans 16 we have record of a number of women servants of Messiah Yeshua in various Congregations.
Phebe v 1-2
Priscilla v. 3-5
Mary, Tryphena, Tryposa, Persis and Julia v 6-15 are mentioned as laborers in the Lord

#5. In Philippians 4:2 Eudios and Syntyche are mentioned as being leaders of the Kahilah of Philippi

#6. Corinthian women prophesied and prayed in the Kahilah (1 Cor 11:4-5). So the scripture in 1 Cor 14;34-35 that is used to condemn women preachers does not refer to preaching but to disturbance in the Kahilah Services- asking or talking out loud to their husbands in the Kahilah as stated in 1 Cor. 14:35. Even so with 1 Tim. 2:11-5 Paul is not condemning women preachers as long as they keep their place and do not "usurp" authority over the man" Both men and women in Corinth were permitted to pray and prophesy, but were regulated by fixed laws in doing so. (1 Cor. 14:24-32)

#7 In 1 Cor 12 Paul compares the Body of Messiah to a human body and mentions 9 gifts of the Spirit/Ruach including the gift of prophecy, for all the members of the Body of Messiah, men and women.

#8 Women were used by God in the Tenach as Prophetesses –(Ex. 15:20, Judges 4:4, 11 Kings 22:14, 11 Chro 34:22, Neh 6:14, Isa 8:3, Lk 1:39-56, Lk 2:36)

The Torah made provisions for women to make sacrifices, attend feasts and make vows.(Deut. 12:11-18, Lev 27)

The Role of Women and their Impact in Traditional Judaism[58]

The role of women in traditional Judaism has been grossly misrepresented and misunderstood. The position of women is not nearly as lowly as many modern people think; in fact, the position of women in halakha (Jewish Law) that dates back to the biblical period is in many ways better than the position of women under US civil law as recently as a century ago.
In traditional Judaism, women's obligations and responsibilities are different from men's, but no less important (in fact, in some ways, women's responsibilities are considered more important, as we shall see).

Both man and women were created in the image of God. According to many Jewish scholars, "man" was created "male and female" (Genesis 1,27) with dual gender, and was later separated into male and female.

According to traditional Judaism, women are endowed with a greater degree of "binah" (intuition, understanding, intelligence) than men. The rabbis inferred this from the idea that women was "built" (Genesis 2,22) rather than "formed" (Genesis 2,7), and the Hebrew root of "build" has the same consonants as the word "binah". It has been said that the matriarchs (Sarah, Rebecca, Rachel, and Leah) were superior to the patriarchs (Abraham, Isaac, and Jacob) in

---

[58] http://www.mechon-Mamre.org/jewfaq/women.htm#Synagogue

prophecy. It has also been said that women did not
participate in the idolatry regarding the golden
calf. Some traditional sources suggest that women are
closer to God's ideal than men.
Women have held positions of respect in Judaism since
biblical times. Miriam is considered one of the liberators
of the people of Israel, along with her brothers Moses
and Aaron. One of the Judges (Deborah) was a
woman. Seven of the 55 prophets of the Bible were
women.

The Ten Commandments require respect for both mother
and father. Note that the father comes first in Exodus
20,11, but the mother comes first in Leviticus 19,3.

There were many learned women of
note. The Talmud and later rabbinical writings speak of
the wisdom of Berurya, the wife of Rabbi Meir. In
several instances, her opinions on halakha (Jewish Law)
were accepted over those of her male contemporaries. In
the ketubah (marriage contract) of Rabbi Akiba's son, the
wife is obligated to teach the husband Torah! Many
rabbis over the centuries have been known to consult
their wives on matters of Jewish law relating to the
women's role, such as laws of kashrut and women's
periods. The wife of a rabbi is referred to as a rebbetzin,
practically a title of her own, which should give some
idea of her significance in Jewish life.

Godly Women and Their Impact During the
Holocaust

I make it a point in my life to study The Holocaust and
the Heroes which include the 6 million men, woman and
children along with millions of others who were
murdered under Hitler's regime. There are hundreds of
women who were not Jewish, who risked their lives to
save the lives of Jewish people even at the risk of their
own lives. These are only a few, but there are hundreds
more who could be listed as well of men and woman
who did what they said "was the right thing to do".
Whenever I read their stories and the stories of those
who survived and those who died, it humbles me and my
prayer is "let me be that brave" when the time comes to
help someone else who is in danger. This is not to
minimize the many men who risked their lives as well,
but to also remember the impact these women had on the
lives that they saved.

One of the women I admire the most is Corrie Ten
Boom. A single woman who along with her family
saved the lives of hundreds of Jews in Holland. She also
had a group of young people who worked along with her,
which was dramatized in the move "Return To The
Hiding Place", who gave their lives in fighting the evil
of Nazism.

DAUGHTERS OF ISRAEL AND THEIR IMPACT IN GODS
KINGDOM PAST, PRESENT AND FUTURE

Corrie Ten Boom[59]

Cornelia "Corrie" ten Boom (15 April 1892 – 15 April
1983) was a Dutch watchmaker and Christian who,
along with her father and other family members, helped
many Jews escape the Nazi Holocaust during World War
II. She was imprisoned for her actions. Her most famous
book, *The Hiding Place*, describes the ordeal.

World War II

In May 1940, the Nazis invaded the Netherlands. Among
their restrictions was banning a club which Ten Boom
had run for young girls.[In May 1942 a well-dressed
women came to the Ten Booms' with a suitcase in hand
and told them that she was a Jew, her husband had been
arrested several months before, her son had gone into
hiding, and Occupation authorities had recently visited
her, so she was afraid to go back. She had heard that the
Ten Booms had helped their Jewish neighbors, the Weils,
and asked if they might help her too. Casper ten Boom
readily agreed that she could stay with them. A devoted
reader of the Old Testament, he believed that the Jews

---

[59] Boom, Corrie ten. The Hiding Place. Peabody Massachusetts
Hendrickson Publishers, 2009
Boom, Corrie ten. The Hiding Place. Peabody Massachusetts Hendrickson
Publishers, 2009, p. 88
"H2G2", DNA, The British Broadcasting Company.
Boom, Corrie ten. The Hiding Place. Peabody Massachusetts Hendrickson
Publishers, 2009, p. 92
*Holocaust Memorial - Corrie ten Boom, The Holocaust Memorial*Boom,
Corrie ten. The Hiding Place. Peabody Massachusetts Hendrickson
Publishers, 2009, p 240
Lessard, William O. The Complete Book of Bananas. Place of Publication
Not Identified: W.O. Lessar1992. Print.

193 | P a g e
193 | P a g e

were the 'chosen people', and he told the women, "In this
household, God's people are always welcome."[2] The
family then became very active in the Dutch
underground hiding refugees; they honored the
Jewish Sabbath.

Thus the Ten Booms began "the hiding place", or "de
schuilplaats", as it was known in Dutch (also known as
"de Béjé", pronounced in Dutch as 'bayay', an
abbreviation of their street address, the Barteljorisstraat).
Corrie and Betsie opened their home to refugees — both
Jews and others who were members of the resistance
movement — being sought by the Gestapoand its Dutch
counterpart. They had plenty of room, although wartime
shortages meant that food was scarce. Every non-Jewish
Dutch person had received a ration card, the requirement
for obtaining weekly food coupons. Through her
charitable work, Ten Boom knew many people in
Haarlem and remembered a couple who had a disabled
daughter. The father was a civil servant who by then was
in charge of the local ration-card office. She went to his
house one evening, and when he asked how many ration
cards she needed, "I opened my mouth to say, 'Five,'"
Ten Boom wrote in *The Hiding Place*. "But the number
that unexpectedly and astonishingly came out instead
was: 'One hundred.'"[4] He gave them to her and she
provided cards to every Jew she met.

Arrest, detention, and release
On February 28, 1944, a Dutch informant named Jan
Vogel told the Nazis about the ten Booms' work; at
around 12:30 the Nazis arrested the entire ten Boom

family. They were sent to <u>Scheveningen</u> prison; Nollie
and Willem were released immediately along with
Corrie's nephew Peter; Casper died 10 days later. The six
people hidden by the ten Booms, among them both Jews
and resistance workers, remained undiscovered. Several
days after the raid resistance workers transferred them to
other locations. Altogether, the Gestapo arrested some 30
people in the ten Boom family home that day.

Corrie and Betsie were sent from Scheveningen
to <u>Herzogenbusch</u> political <u>concentration camp</u> (also
known as Kamp Vught), and finally to the <u>Ravensbrück
concentration camp</u>, a woman's labor camp in <u>Germany</u>.
There they held worship services, after the hard days at
work, using a Bible that they had managed to sneak in.
After her health continued to recede, Betsie died on
December 16, 1944 with a smile on her lips. Before she
died, she told Corrie, "There is no pit so deep that He
[God] is not deeper still."

Life after the war

After the war, ten Boom returned to The Netherlands to
set up a <u>rehabilitation</u> center. The refugee houses
consisted of concentration-camp survivors and sheltered
the jobless Dutch who previously collaborated with
Germans during the Occupation. She returned to
Germany in 1946, and traveled the world as a public
speaker, appearing in more than 60 countries. She wrote
many books during this time.

Irene Sendler[60] Another woman with an incredible story.

Irena Sendlerowa, a Polish woman who smuggled thousands of children out of the Warsaw Ghetto saving them from certain death at the hands of the Nazis, died at the age of 98.

As a social worker, she had neither the financial might nor the contact book of Oskar Schindler, to whom she is almost inevitably compared, yet she rescued almost double the number of children, about 2,500 in total.

The tricks of her trade were not elaborate: tool boxes, trolleys, suitcases and old sewer pipes were used to smuggle Jewish babies and toddlers out of the ghetto, undetected by the Nazis.

"Her courageous activities ... serve as a beacon of light to the world, inspiring hope and restoring faith in the innate goodness of mankind," said Avner Shalev, the chairman of Israel's Holocaust memorial center, Yad Vashem.

---

[60] Yitta Halberstam & Judith Leventhal, *Small Miracles of the Holocaust*, The Lyons Press; 1st edition (13 August 2008), ISBN 978-1-59921-407-8

Richard Lkas, Forgotten Survivors: Polish Christians Remember the Nazi Occupation ISBN 978-0-7006-1350-2

Anna Mieszkowska, IRENA SENDLER Mother of the Holocaust Children Publisher: Praeger; Tra edition (18 November 2010) Language: English ISBN 978-0-313-38593-3

Mordecai Paldiel, *The Path of the Righteous: Gentile Rescuers of Jews During the Holocaust*, Ktav Publishing House (January 1993), ISBN 9780881253764

Irene Tomaszewski & Tecia Werblowski, *Zegota: The Council to Aid Jews in Occupied Poland 1942–1945*, Price-Patterson, ISBN 1-896881-15-7

Nominated for Nobel Peace Prize
Officially recognized as a national hero by the Polish
parliament last year as well as being nominated for a
Nobel Peace Prize.
"People who stand up for others, for the weak, are very
rare," Marek Edelman, the last surviving commander of
the Warsaw Ghetto Uprising, told Polish television. "The
world would have been a better place if there were more
of them."

Courageous Women and Children of the Holocaust[61]

Survivors of the Holocaust are often described as
courageous. But, it only takes a limited amount of
courage to save your own life because the will to live is
inherent in all humans and all animals.

The truly courageous are the rescuers -- the ones who
risked their own lives, the lives of their families or their
own comfort or status to help save the lives of others.
It was not easy. Many of the rescuers would die if one of
their neighbors found out. Even your own neighbor
could turn you in to be executed. It was also not
fashionable -- not the thing to do. It was much easier to
look the other way and say, "What can I do?"

In Poland, it was a crime punishable by execution if you
or anyone in your family was suspected of aiding a Jew.

---

[61] http://www.holocaustforgotten.com/realcourage.htm

There was no court or trial. Executions were done
quickly and publicly -- with no regard to right or wrong.

Most rescuers are NOT listed at Yad Vashem. Why? The
Jewish memorial known as *Righteous of the Nations* has
very strict guidelines for inclusion in their famous list.
Testimony of witnesses is mandatory. But, many rescuers
died alone. Many courageous rescuers failed to save the
lives of their Jewish families. Sometimes entire rescuer
families and all witnesses were executed. There were
also thousands of anonymous rescuers -- people who
helped secretly and quietly but were never recognized.
Yad Vashem's venerable list only includes a small
percentage of the actual rescuers.

The Women - Their Capabilities Underestimated

Many women were left alone at home while their men
fought in the streets and forests. Because of the inherent
nature of the female, many women became heroines ten
times over.

Who would have suspected, "Babcza", the old lady, her
head covered with a brightly flowered babushka, selling
apples from a cart of being a secret liaison for the
underground resistance movement? One pocket of her
apron held coins for making change, but the other pocket
held cryptic messages that she passed to a young man
who uttered the correct coded words.

The Destruction of Crematorium Number Four[62]
Be Strong and Brave by Roza Robota

Women liaisons were involved in another significant act
of resistance at Auschwitz. The setting was the Union
Werke factory, which manufactured V2 rockets parts.
Only female inmates were selected to labor there. One
room of the plant, the Pulverraum, was the only place at
Auschwitz where prisoners had access to gunpowder.
There, nine young women worked, handling the explosive
material for the manufacture of trigger caps.

A plot was devised by Sonderkommandos to obtain the
gunpowder from the Pulverraum. Through a series of
links including prisoners Rosa Robota and Alla Gaertner,
the "Sondermen" asked the women in the trigger cap
factory to smuggle gunpowder to them. All of the women
accepted the challenge, including Gaertner, the leader of
the gunpowder unit. Among others who worked in the
factory were Regina Saperstein, Anna Heilman and Rose
Meth. Meth wrote of the event:
In March 1943, Estusia approached me. She told me that
resistance was being organized and we were in a position
to help because we were the only ones who had access to
gunpowder. Would I be willing to risk the danger of
being caught? Of course, I agreed right away because it
gave me a way to fight back. I felt very good about it and
I didn't care about the danger. None of us did.[82]
The young women smuggled out minute amounts of
gunpowder in their mess tins (fitted with double bottoms),

---

[62] http://www.theverylongview.com/WATH/essays/courier11.htm

in the knots of the scarves in their hair, and in the seams and folds of their dresses. One of the conspirators of this undertaking, Anna Heilman wrote:

Inside our dresses we had what we called a little boit'l, a pocket, and the biot'l was where everybody hid their little treasures, wrapped in pieces of cloth. Often there were searches. When they conducted searches we used to untie the string and spill the gunpowder behind us on the ground so it wouldn't be found.[83]

Three women could accumulate approximately three teaspoons of powder in one day. Once successfully smuggled out of the factory the gunpowder was handed off, according to Anna Heilman, "through Marta to Antichka who was working in Birkenau. She ran between Auschwitz and Birkenau and gave it to Roza Robota."[84]

Roza Robota was a survivor of the transport of Jews from Ciechanow where she had been a member of Ha-Shomer Ha-tza'ir. She was the only member of her family not to have been gassed upon arrival at Auschwitz in November of 1942. Forced to labor in the Bekleidungskommando unit where confiscated clothing and personal possessions of prisoners were sorted, she organized a resistance group which distributed news obtained by the camp underground organization from radio broadcasts.

Roza made the initial contact with several women in the Schwartzpulver factory, who were also native to Ciechanow. Despite the dangers and difficulties the women agreed to steal the gunpowder.

Once it was smuggled outside the Union Werke the women passed the explosive material to Roza and

Hadassa Zlotnicka who gave it to Asir-Godel Zilber, another native of Ciechanow. Zilber passed the contraband on to a member of the Sonderkommando and then the material finally reached the Russian "Sondermen," who fashioned the gunpowder into grenades and bombs. It took the women over a year to smuggle enough gunpowder to realize the conspiracy's goal: to destroy one of the crematoria. The finished explosives were buried near the crematoria until the proper time. On October 7, 1944 the Sondermen recovered the explosives and detonated Crematorium Number IV, putting it permanently out of commission.

Initially, the possibility that women could be involved in transferring explosives was inconceivable to the Gestapo, but eventually their investigation led to Alla Gaertner, Roza Robota, and the Pulverraum plant. Four women in the conspiracy were tortured and murdered: Robota, Gaertner, Regina Saperstein and Estusia. None of them betrayed their fellow conspirators. One of the leaders of the plot, Noah Zabladowicz, a member of the Jewish underground in the camp, stole a brief visit with Robota in punishment Block 11 before her death. She had endured torture, mutilation and lay dying on the floor of her cell. Roza urged Zabladowicz to encourage the members of the Auschwitz underground to continue their work. Her last message was a note scratched on a piece of paper smuggled from her cell: "Hazak V'Amatz: Be Strong and Brave."[85] Roza Robota was twenty-three.
The remaining heroines who smuggled the gunpowder were forced to watch the hangings of their co-conspirators who all yelled Zemsta! (Revenge!) before their execution.

MIEP GIES
MOVIE: Anne Frank: The Whole Story, Diary of Anne
Frank, etc.
BOOK: *Anne Frank Remembered*
STORY: Anne Frank is known for writing her (now best-
selling) diary in a secret annex. Although she did not
survive the Holocaust (she died in Bergen-Belsen),
Frank's father survived and he published her diary. Gies
was one of the Frank family's many helpers. In 1933 she
worked for Anne's father, Otto, and became a close
family friend. She kept Anne's diary, although she never
read it until she turned them over to Otto Frank.

IRENE GUT OPDYKE
BOOK: *In My Hands* by Irene Gut, memoir
STORY: Young Polish nurse Irene Gut Opdyke hid 12
Jews – in a Nazi officer's house. She notes things started
at small, as she first began smuggling food into the local
ghetto. She later began smuggling Jews into the woods,
and finally found a job in a Nazi officer's house and
began hiding Jews there. Although a movie was going to
be made about her life, it hit lots of controversy.

SEFANIA AND HELENE PODGORSKA
MOVIE: Hidden in Silence (Lifetime TV movie)
BOOK: Featured in *Women Heroes of World War II* by
Kathryn Atwood
STORY: Two Polish sisters, a teen and 7 year old child,
hide 13 Jews in their attic for 2.5 years.

DIET AND SIETSMA, HEIN EMAN
MOVIE: The Reckoning (Documentary about the Dutch resistance, featuring Diet)
BOOK: Memoir, *Things We Couldn't Say*
PODCAST: Focus on the Family: God's Grace is Sufficient
STORY: Dutch Christian resistance worker Diet Eman proves that faith, hope, and love really do conquer all. From helping a few Jewish friends to being arrested for a false visa, Diet Eman has an amazing story of courage and faith. Her fiancé also played an amazing part in this, paying with his life and regretting nothing. I would highly recommend reading her memoir and listening to her tell her story on Focus on the Family.[63]

SOPHIA SCHOLL
Sophia Scholl was a German student, who was active in the White Rose – a non-violent resistance group to Hitler and the Nazi party. In 1943, she was caught delivering anti-war propaganda and, with her brother Hans Scholl, was executed for high treason.
She has become an important symbol of anti-Nazi resistance in Germany.

Sophie was an avid reader and developed an interest in philosophy and theology. She developed a strong Christian faith which emphasized the basic dignity of every human being. This religious faith proved an important cornerstone of her opposition to the

---

[63] http://lechaimontheright.com/2014/06/18-righteous-holocaust-rescuers-movies-memoirs.html

increasingly all-pervading Nazi ideology of German society. Sophie also developed a talent for art – drawing and painting, and she became acquainted with artistic circles which, in Nazi terms, were labelled degenerate. The White Rose was an informal group who sought to oppose the war and Nazi regime. It was founded in early 1942 by Hans Scholl, Willia Graf and Christoph Probst. They wrote six anti-Nazi resistance leaflets and distributed them across Munich. Initially Sophie was not aware of the group, but when she found out her brother's activities, she was keen to take part. Sophie took part in distributing leaflets and carrying messages. As a woman, she was less likely to be stopped by the SS.

Reports of mass killings of Jews, were also widely shared amongst members of the White Rose. This features in the second White Rose pamphlet.

" Since the conquest of Poland 300,000 Jews have been murdered, a crime against human dignity…Germans encourage fascist criminals if no chord within them cries out at the sight of such deeds. An end in terror is preferable to terror without end."
Sophie Scholl and other members of the White Rose remain a potent symbol of how people can take a courageous action to resist, even the most brutal totalitarian regime.[64]

---

[64] Citation : Pettinger, Tejvan. "Biography of Sophie Scholl ", Oxford, UK .

The Prejudice We Face and How Will We Impact Future Generations of Women?

Woman of Faith Caught in the Middle [65] by John D. Garr page 15

"The majority of church woman, however are caught in the middle between restrictive requirements of the past that continue to be staunchly defended in the present and the demands of women's liberationists that have echoed across society for over a century and have created clouds of dust in the pristine sanctuaries of the church. Godly women have an unwavering commitment to godliness, to adhering to the principles of conduct that they know instinctively must be taught by Holy Scripture. They cannot bring themselves to jettison the Bible as a relic of an antiquated patriarchal male God in order to accommodate the demands of feminists. They know intuitively, however, that something is wrong with the historical church's positions on woman that still carry over into the present to one degree or another. Surely these positions do not reflect God's eternal will for woman.

At the same time, women are often bidden by an inner calling of the Holy Spirit to roles that have been traditionally forbidden to woman. Divine charismata create open doors for Spirits-directed actions: "A Persons gift makes room for him (her)" Proverbs 18:16.

---

[65] God and Woman, John D. Garr Golden Key Press Page. 15
Copyright 2011 by John D. Garr

When those to whom these gifts have been given by the
Spirit are feminine in gender, however, inhibitions cloud
the issue, imposing spiritual and psychological
constraints. No godly woman wants to be a "Jezebel",
nor does she want to be viewed as one; therefore, most
who receive charismata (gifts of the spirit) become
shrinking violets, adorned with the beauty of divine
calling but afraid to stand out in the light of day"

As one who has been in leadership positions for over 35
years, I can tell you the road has not been easy to
become a woman Rabbi heading a Congregation along
with my husband. It is hard feeling the call of God
within you to teach and minister to people, only to be
turned away because you are a woman.

We are not a majority, but a minority who want to join
the ranks of other great women of God and our only
desire is to make an impact for His Kingdom.

There are many challenges we face:

- Prejudice
- False accusations
- Intimidation
- Rejection
- Misunderstood
- Not taken seriously
- The fine line we walk
- Keeping our femininity in a man's world
- Husbands whose wives are ministers and in the
limelight

DAUGHTERS OF ISRAEL AND THEIR IMPACT IN GODS
KINGDOM PAST, PRESENT AND FUTURE

Let's look at these challenges one at a time.

Prejudice:

Called and anointed but not allowed to speak. At times,
we are made to feel like we need to apologize for
wanting to serve God and teach others to do so as well. I
remember when I was single and in leadership. I knew
many single men who were in ministry also and did not
like the fact that a was a strong woman spiritually and a
minister. One even told me the women he marries, that
her ministry will be him. I was not considered the ideal
choice for a wife because of my call to be a minister in
the pulpit (so to speak). I did eventually meet someone
who was not afraid of my anointing but blessed by it as
well.

Many times, he has faced the same ridicule as well with
comments such as:

Why is your wife teaching and not you?
Why do you allow her to lead a Congregation?
What kind of man are you that lets his wife teach?

One time after one of the Conferences that I hosted and
put together an irate man who attended the conference
and was blessed by the speakers emailed me and said;
"You need to change the name of your ministry, how
dare you call it Deborah's Messianic Ministries after
yourself. In reality it was not named after me but after
Deborah in the Bible, but he went on to say "You need to

207 | P a g e

shut up and let your husband teach" It didn't matter to
him that my husband was not called to teach, but
evangelize! My husband and I are a team, however my
job is more public, where his job is more behind the
scenes, yet we work as one.

**Here are some quotes by "Church Fathers" regarding
Women.**

Church Doctors and Fathers

Women is a temple built over a sewer. *–Tertullian, "the
father of Latin Christianity" (c160-225)*
[Women's] very consciousness of their own nature must
evoke feelings of shame.*–Saint Clement of Alexandria,
Christian theologian (c150-215): Pedagogues II, 33, 2*
Nor are the women to smear their faces with the
ensnaring devices of wily cunning. . . The Instructor
[Christ] orders them to go forth "in becoming apparel,
and adorn themselves with shamefacedness and sobriety,
subject to their own husbands." *–Saint Clement of
Alexandria, Christian theologian (c150-215):*

 In pain shall you bring forth children, women, and you
shall turn to your husband and he shall rule over you.
And do you not know that you are Eve? God's sentence
hangs still over all your sex and His punishment weighs
down upon you. You are the devil's gateway; you are she
who first violated the forbidden tree and broke the law of
God. It was you who coaxed your way around him
whom the devil had not the force to attack. With what
ease you shattered that image of God: Man! Because of

the death you merited, even the Son of God had to die... Women, you are the gate to hell. *–Tertullian, "the father of Latin Christianity" (c160-225):*

On the Apparel of Women, chapter 1
For it is improper for a woman to speak in an assembly, no matter what she says,
even if she says admirable things, or even saintly things, that is of little
consequence, since they come from the mouth of a woman. *–Origen (d. 258):*

Fragments on First Corinthians, 74
Women does not possess the image of God in herself but only when taken together
with the male who is her head, so that the whole substance is one image. But
when she is assigned the role as helpmate, a function that pertains to her
alone, then she is not the image of God. But as far as the man is concerned, he
is by himself alone the image of God just as fully and completely as when he and
the women are joined together into one. *–Saint Augustine, Bishop of Hippo Regius (354-430)*

What is the difference whether it is in a wife or a mother, it is still Eve the temptress that we must beware of in any women...? I fail to see what use women can be to man, if one excludes the function of bearing children. *–Saint Augustine, Bishop of Hippo Regius (354 – 430): De genesi ad litteram, 9, 5-9*

Women is a misbegotten man and has a faulty and defective nature in comparison to his. Therefore she is unsure in herself. What she cannot get, she seeks to obtain through lying and diabolical deceptions. And so, to put it briefly, one must be on one's guard with every women, as if she were a poisonous snake and the horned devil. … Thus in evil and perverse doings women is cleverer, that is, slyer, than man. Her feelings drive women toward every evil, just as reason impels man toward all good. *–Saint Albertus Magnus, Dominican theologian, 13th century: Quaestiones super de animalibus XV q. 1*

As regards the individual nature, women is defective and misbegotten, for the active force in the male seed tends to the production of a perfect likeness in the masculine sex; while the production of women comes from a defect in the active force or from some material indisposition, or even from some external influence. *–Thomas Aquinas, Doctor of the Church, 13th century: Summa Theologica I q. 92 a. 1*

Protestant Reformers
The word and works of God is quite clear, that women were made either to be wives or prostitutes. *–Martin Luther, Reformer (1483-1546), Works 12.94*

No gown worse becomes a woman than the desire to be wise. *–Martin Luther, Reformer (1483-1546)*

Men have broad and large chests, and small narrow hips, and more understanding than women, who have but small and narrow breasts, and broad hips, to the end they should remain at home, sit still, keep house, and bear and bring up children. *–Martin Luther, Reformer (1483-1546), Table Talk*

Thus, the women, who had perversely exceeded her proper bounds, is forced back to her own position. She had, indeed, previously been subject to her husband, but that was a liberal and gentle subjection; now, however, she is cast into servitude. *–John Calvin, Reformer (1509-1564): Commentary on Genesis, p. 172.*

Do not any longer contend for mastery, for power, money, or praise. Be content to be a private, insignificant person, known and loved by God and me. . . . of what importance is your character to mankind, if you were buried just now Or if you had never lived, what loss would it be to the cause of God. *–John Wesley, founder of Methodist movement (1703-1791): letter to his wife, July 15, 1774*

As Women of God, His Eishes Chayel how do we handle the Prejudice we face with Dignity and Grace?

False Accusations:
Many of us are accused of being feminist, Jezebels, women liber's because we dare to obey God. Of course, as you see above, the seeds of contempt have long been

sown into the minds of Christians and other faiths
regarding women in ministry.

Intimidation:

We need to prove ourselves above and beyond our male
counterparts. I have great respect for the great men of
God who I have served under. I have great respect for
the Rabbis I serve under now, and I understand what it
means to be submissive to authority.

Many times, we have been bullied if we dare to teach
others the Word of God. However, we need to obey the
call that God has put on our lives as long as we keep our
lives in God's order.

Rejection:

Unfortunately, as women, our ideas and input are often
rejected or not taken seriously. We see this in all areas of
life, even in our homes.

We cannot allow a spirit of rejection set in, or a spirit of
anger, this is what the enemy wants. We need to walk in
a higher level of spirituality and trust in the Father's call.

Misunderstood:

How many times have strong women been labeled as
Jezebels because God has blessed them with leadership
qualities? Or being accused that we are trying to usurp a
man's' authority.

Being a woman called to leadership is a much tougher
position then when a man is in a leadership position. We

need to keep our lives and homes in balance and show
ourselves to truly be women who only want to serve
God.

Not Being Taken Seriously:
I don't know how many times I have taught on a topic
only to hear someone extol the teaching of a male
counterpart teaching and saying the same thing.

The Fine Line We Walk:
We need to constantly be on guard so that pride does not
get a hold of us or bitterness. We need to keep our
spiritual lives in order and our homes. We need to make
sure that we never bring a reproach on the Name of God
because of actions that are not considered proper for a
woman.

We have to avoid self-pity when we experience all of the
above realizing that the only approval we need to be
concerned about is God's.

Keeping our Femininity in a Man's world
As women we have a unique perspective, we have been
blessed with deeper spiritual incite and discernment and
the heart of a mother.

We do not have to act like a man in order to be accepted.
If we are anointed and speak forth the truth, then those
who have discerning hearts will take heed to our words
and teaching.

Husbands who have Wives who are Rabbis
When God calls one, he calls another so in reality they
both share in the leadership but in different ways. It is
important to make sure that your husband is a vital part
of what God has called you to do and that he is made to
feel a part of this calling.

Daughters of Israel and Their Impact on the Future
We have looked at the Daughters of Israel Past and
Present, but what about the future?

We have been given many wonderful role models in the
Bible and in History of women who answered God's call
in spite of the prejudice and pressure from those we
serve.

However, there is no running from this call because it
burns inside of you so strongly that you cannot run from
you, so just run to it.

I have been in ministry for 40 years so I have some
experience of the struggle it takes to be a woman called
by God. However, I kept praying and seeking God and
He sent Godly men into my life who say the anointing
and the call to teach and encouraged it and treated me as
an equal in God's work.

We need to continually strive to be God's Eishes Chayil,
Virtuous Women and just continue to persevere until the
end.

We need to rest in fact, that God loves us and has restored us in Messiah Yeshua and it is better to obey God than man, when man comes against God's plans and purposes for our lives.

May He raise up many more Sarah's, Rebecca's, Leah's, Deborah's, Ruth's and Esther's to name a few who will make an impact on his kingdom during the time that they have been allotted here on earth.

In Conclusion:
I hope that my life will leave an impact on my children and children's children and all of those I have been privileged to serve.

In this paper I, have attempted to prove that women have made a great impact in this world. Ha Satan hates women because from the very beginning, God promised to bring the redeemer through a woman to redeem mankind.

Thus, women have been persecuted greatly in the past and continue to face prejudice, especially in the realm of ministry. However, despite it all, women have made a great impact in Gods Kingdom, plans and purposes.

Bibliography

Daughter of Destiny – Women who revolutionized
Jewish life and Torah Education – Complied by Devora
Rubin Me'sorah Publications, ltd. Copyright 1988, 2001

The Eishes Chayil Haggadah – Rabbi Dov Weller,
Artscroll Me'sorah Publications, ltd. Copyright 2016

Feminine by Design – The God Fashioned Women –
John D. Garr PH.D. Golden Key Press, Atlanta Georgia
Copyright 2012

God and Women – Women in God's Image & Likeness –
John D. Garr- Golden Key Press. Atlanta Georgia –
Copyright 2011

No Greater Treasure – Stories of Extraordinary Women
Drawn from the Talmud and Midrash- Shoshana Lepon ,
Targum Press- Copyright 1990

The Sacred Calling – Four Decades of Women in the
Rabbinate – Rabbi Rebecca Einstein Shorr and Rabbi
Alysa Mendelson Graf, Editors CCAR Press Copyright
2016 Central Conference of American Rabbis

She Shall Be Praised-The Faith and Courage of
extraordinary women – Avraham Erlanger, Me'sorah
Publishers, ltd Copyright 1999

Women's Wisdom – The Garden of Peace for Women –
Rabbi Shalom Arush, Chut Shel Chessed Institutions,
Copyright 2010

Women's Prayer Siddur – Artscroll Publishers

Articles

Jewish Encyclopedia.com

Jewish Pathways – Women In The Bible – Dina
Coppersmith

Mother Love Among The Flocks Rabbi Monica
Lowenstein, NY
Shalomyshua@aol.com

Paul's View of Women in Positions of Church
Leadership By Lenore Lindsey Mullican
The Role of Women in the Assembly – Tim Hegg
Copyright 1992 Torah Resources.com

Women In Judaism A Study – Rabbitzin Mrs. Leah
Kohen
 The JPS Guide to Jewish Women: 600 B.C.E–1900 C.E.
Philadelphia: The Jewish Publication Society Taitz, E.,
Henry, S., & Tallan, C. (2003).

10 Lies The Church Tells Women – J. Lee Grady

International Encyclopedia of Women
http://www.internationalstandardbible.com/W/women.ht
ml
Paul's View of Women in Positions of Church
Leadership By Lenore Lindsey Mullican

DAUGHTERS OF ISRAEL AND THEIR IMPACT IN GODS
KINGDOM PAST, PRESENT AND FUTURE

Endnotes

---

[i] **Page 8 Jewish Identity** According to the Mishnah, the first written source for halakha, the status of the offspring of mixed marriages was determined matrilineally.

According to historian Shaye J. D. Cohen, in the Bible, the status of the offspring of mixed marriages was determined patrilineally. He brings two likely explanations for the change in Mishnaic times: first, the Mishnah may have been applying the same logic to mixed marriages as it had applied to other mixtures (*kilayim*). Thus, a mixed marriage is forbidden as is the union of a horse and a donkey, and in both unions the offspring are judged matrilineally. Second, the Tannaim may have been influenced by Roman law, which dictated that when a parent could not contract a legal marriage, offspring would follow the mother.[20]

According to *halakha*, to determine a person's Jewish status (Hebrew: *yuhasin*) one needs to consider the status of both parents. If both parents are Jewish, their child will also be considered Jewish, and the child takes the status of the father (e.g., as a kohen). If either parent is subject to a genealogical disability (e.g., is a mamzer) then the child is also subject to that disability. If one of the parents is not Jewish, the rule is that the child takes the status of the mother (Kiddushin 68b, Shulchan Aruch, EH 4:19).[23] The ruling is derived from various sources including Deuteronomy 7:1–5, Leviticus 24:10, Ezra 10:2–3.[23] Accordingly, if the mother is Jewish, so is her child, and if she is not Jewish, neither is

---

her child considered Jewish. In Orthodox Judaism the child of a non-Jewish mother can be considered Jewish only by a process of conversion to Judaism.[24] The child is also freed from any disabilities and special status to which the father may have been subject (e.g., being a mamzer or kohen) under Jewish law.[25]

The Orthodox and Conservative branches of Judaism maintain that the halakhic rules (i.e. matrilineal descent) are valid and binding. Reform and Liberal Judaism do not accept the halakhic rules as binding, and most branches accept a child of one Jewish parent, whether father or mother, as Jewish if the parents raise the child as a Jew and foster a Jewish identity in the child, noting that "in the Bible the line always followed the father, including the cases of Joseph and Moses, who married into non-Israelite priestly families."[26] (However, according to the oral tradition of Orthodox Judaism, the spouses of both Joseph and Moses converted to Judaism prior to marrying them.) The Reform movement's standard states that "for those beyond childhood claiming Jewish identity, other public acts or declarations may be added or substituted after consultation with their rabbi".[27] Advocates of patrilineal descent point to Genesis 48:15–20 and Deuteronomy 10:15.[28] This policy is commonly known as patrilineal descent, though "bilineal" would be more accurate.
https://en.wikipedia.org/wiki/Who_is_a_Jew%3F

ii Sarah, Hannah, Abigail, and Esther are never called prophetesses in the Hebrew Bible. Thus, the Rabbis had

---

to explain the reasons they called these four women
prophetesses.

Sarah is called a prophetess "because she discerned
[*sakethah*] by means of the holy spirit, as it is said, In all
that Sarah saith unto thee, hearken to her voice. Another
explanation is: because all gazed [*sakin*] at her beauty."

Hannah is called a prophetess because "Hannah prayed
and said, My heart exulteth in the Lord, my horn is
exalted in the Lord. [She said], 'my horn is exalted', and
not, 'my cruse is exalted', thus implying that the royalty
of [the hour of] David and Solomon, who were anointed
from a horn, would be prolonged, but the royalty of [the
house of] Saul and Jehu, who were anointed with a
cruse, would not be prolonged."

The views about Abigail appear at the end
of *Megillah* 14a and at the beginning of *Megillah* 14b.
Abigail is declared to be a prophetess because she
declared that David would be a great king in the near
future. According to the Talmud, Abigail said to David:
"your fame is not yet spread abroad in the world. . . .
When she left him she said to him, and when the Lord
shall have done good to my lord . . . then remember thy
handmaid."
Esther is called a prophetess because "it is written, Now
it came to pass on the third day that Esther clothed
herself in royalty. Surely it should say, 'royal apparel'?
What it shows is that the holy spirit clothed her. It is
written here, 'and she clothed.'"

The Rabbis were not limited in their view that the Holy Spirit could use a woman to prophesy. It is possible that many nameless women also prophesied in Israel. These female voices remain unheard and undiscovered for unknown reasons. And they may remain silenced forever because their society failed to recognize that they too were called and sent by a God who does not discriminate because of gender. (Dr. Claude Mariottini, Professor of Old Testament)

[iii]   **SARAI** (Sĕr' ī) Personal name meaning "princess." Wife and half sister of Abraham (Gen. 11:29–25:10). Sarah, first called Sarai, had the same father as Abraham. Marriages with half brothers were not uncommon in her time. Sarah traveled with Abraham from Ur to Haran. Then at the age of 65 she accompanied him to Canaan as Abraham followed God's leadership in moving to the land God had promised. During a famine in Canaan, Abraham and Sarah fled to Egypt. This was Abraham's first attempt to pass off Sarah as his sister rather than wife because he feared that he would be killed when the Egyptians saw Sarah's beauty. Consequently, the Pharaoh thought Sarah was Abraham's sister, took Sarah into court, and treated Abraham well. When the Lord sent serious disease on Pharaoh's household, he saw the deception and sent them away. The second trick about Abraham's relationship with Sarah was in the court of Abimelech, king of Gerar, who also took in Sarah. God intervened in Abimelech's dream and protected Sarah. He sent them away with the right to live there and with a gift for Sarah.[iii]

In her grief over her barrenness, Sarah gave her maid
Hagar to Abraham in the hope of an heir, but she
expressed resentment when Hagar conceived. When
Sarah was almost 90 years old, God changed her name
and promised her a son. A year later she bore Isaac.

At the age of 127, Sarah died at Hebron, where she
was buried in the cave in the field of Machpelah near
Mamre.

[iv] "Paul's view of Women in Positions of Church Leadership"

[v] 1 William David Spencer, "The Chaining of the
Church," *Christian History* VII, no. 1 (1988), p. 25.

2 Randy Petersen, "What About Paul?" *Christian
History* VII, no. 1 (1988)p. 27.

3 Krister Stendahl, *Paul Among Jews and
Gentiles* (Philadelphia: Fortress Press, 1976), p. 7.

4 Pinchas Lapide and Peter Stuhlmacher, *Paul: Rabbi
and Apostle* (Minneapolis: Augsburg Publishing House,
1984), p. 47.

5 G. Bilezikian, *Beyond Sex Roles* (Grand Rapids Book
House, 1985), p. 26

6 m. Sotah 1:9.

7 *The Wycliffe Bible Commentary* (Chicago: Moody
Press, 1962), p. 418.

8 Rachel Levine, "The Women's Role: Part I," *Yavo Digest* 5, no. 1 (1991), p. 18.

9 Gretchen Gaebelein Hull, *Equal to Serve* (New Jersey: Fleming H. Revell, 1987), p. 113.

10 A. Cohen, *Everyman' s Talmud* (New York: Schocken Books, 1975), p. 159.

11 "Women," *Encyclopedia Judiaca*, Corrected Edition. (Jerusalem: Keter, 1972)

12 Rachel D. Levine, "The Women's Role: Part II," *Yavo Digest* 5, no. 1 (1991), p. 4.

13 b. Pesahim 62b.

14 H. Freedman, trans., I. Epstein, ed., b. Pesahim 62b. (note)

15 m. Kiddushin 1:7.

16 b. Menahoth 43b.

17 Cohen, 159.

18 C. G. Montefiore and H. Loewe, *A Rabbinic Anthology* (New York: Schocken Books, 1974), p. 658.

19 Shmuel Safrai, "The Role of Women in the Temple" *Jerusalem Perspective* 2, no. 9 (1989), p. 5.

20 m. Tamid 5:1.

21 Safrai, 6.

22 Bernadette J. Brooten, *Women Leaders in the Ancient Synagogue* (Chico, CA: Scholars' Press, 1982), p. 104.

23 Rachel D. Levine, "Women in First Century Judaism," *Yavo Digest* 1, no. 4 (1987), p. 7.

24 Levine, 7.

25 m. Berahot 3:3.

26 b. Sotah 22a.

27 Brooten, 142.

28 Brooten, 5-99.

29 m. Avoth 1:4.

30 Rachel D. Levine, "Women Disciples," *Yavo Digest* 1, no. 5 (1987), p. 4.

31 William Arndt and Wilbur Gingrich, *A Greek-English Lexicon of the New Testament and Other Early Christian Literature* (Chicago: University of Chicago, 1979), p. 787.

32 Henry C. Liddell and Robert Scott, *A Greek-English Lexicon* (Oxford: Clarendon, 1985), p. 1711.

33 Ruth A. Tucker and Walter Liefeld, *Daughers of the Church*, (Grand Rapids: Zondervan, 1987), p. 69.

34 Arndt and Gingrich, p. 99.

35 Tucker and Liefeld, p. 73.

36Catherine Kroeger, "The Neglected History of Women in the Early Church," *Christian History* VII, no. 1 (1988), p. 7.

37 Arndt and Gingrich, p. 99.

38 Abraham Even-Shoshan, *HaMilon HaChadash* (Jerusalem: Kiryath Sepher, 1975), p. 2706.

39 Liddell and Scott, p. 1526.

40 Elisabeth Schussler Fiorenza, "Word, Spirit and Power:

Women in Early Christian Communities," *Women of Spirit*, ed.

Rosemary Ruether and Eleanor McLaughlin (New York: Simon and

Schuster, 1979), p. 36.

41 Catherine Kroeger, "The Apostle Paul and the Greco-Roman Cults of Women," *Journal of the Evangelical Theological Society*, March, 1987), p. 25.

Made in the USA
Monee, IL
18 May 2023

33920323R00128